AF407425

MESMERIZE

When Heaven & Earth Collide

DAVID EDWARDS

Mystify Series | Book 2

SOR

Copyright

Copyright © 2022 David Edwards
Mesmerize: When Heaven & Earth Collide
"Mystify Series: Book Two"
1st Edition: July 17th, 2022
(September, 2022 Update)
ISBN: 9798839760790
School of Revivalists Ministries Inc
schoolofrevivalists.com

All rights reserved. No part of this book may be used or reproduced by any means, graphic, electronic, or mechanical, including photocopying, recording, taping or by an information storage retrieval system without the written permission of the author except in the case of brief quotations embodied in critical articles and reviews. Because of the dynamic nature of the internet, any web address or links contained in this book may have changed since the publication and may no longer be valid.

Cover Image: Canva

Scripture quotations marked TPT are from The Passion Translation®. Copyright © 2017, 2018 by Passion & Fire Ministries, Inc. Used by permission. All rights reserved. ThePassionTranslation.com.

Scripture quotations marked (ESV) are taken from The Holy Bible, English Standard Version® (ESV®), copyright © 2001 by Crossway, a publishing ministry of Good News Publishers. Used by permission. All rights reserved.

Scripture quotations marked (Berean) are taken from The Holy Bible, Berean Study Bible, BSB. Copyright ©2016, 2020 by Bible Hub. Used by Permission. All Rights Reserved Worldwide.

Scripture quotations marked "KJV" are taken from the Holy Bible, King James Version, Cambridge, 1769.

ENDORSEMENTS

In the book, *Mesmerize: When Heaven & Earth Collide*, by David Edwards, you will learn that atmospheres are transformed through the sound of God's creation. David brings to light that Jesus is the very note from the Father's heart given to us. He shows how Jesus restored creation's sound to His Father's frequency and how to recognize His sound in us and creation. David says, "We then become His tuning fork, harmonizing creation back to Himself." Your heart will be opened to be transformed, and to understand how "lovesick the Father is for those who are lovesick for Him." This book is a MUST READ for anyone wanting to experience more of The Presence of His Glory.

Donna Grisham
Founder & President, Journeys of Choice Ministries
Host of The Real Pro-Choice Show, ISN & METV
Author, *Journeys of Choice*

From my personal experiences, I find it impossible to read about such glorious encounters with Jesus as described by David Edwards in *Mesmerize* without being pulled into the secret place of seeking His face. There's an oil and substance on this book that is a byproduct of being an eyewitness to the beautiful collision of Heaven and Earth throughout multiple decades. There's so much to discover in the realm of the Spirit and David provokes a hunger for the more of God. These pages are filled with extraordinary invitations to journey in the family of God. *Mesmerize* is by far one of the most entertaining, life-changing, and Jesus-revealing books I have ever read.

Tabatha Wade
Founder, P3 Prayer House
Author, *The ABCs of Ascension*

Seriously, who wants a God who can fit predictably Who wants a God who can fit predictably within the limits of our finite brain's capacity? How could a loving, outside-the-box God send His only Son to die for us and yet want us to live inside a box of what humans can do ourselves? Why would an eternal God give us our five senses for only this world instead of designing them as portals for learning to rule and reign in His now-but-not-yet-for-us eternal Kingdom? In *Mesmerize*, David Edwards dares to challenge our mundane, small thinking about God by sharing glimpses of Heaven touching earth beyond our wildest imagination. As you read, dare to believe the veil between heaven and earth is thinner than we ever imagined. Your "here and now" can be a playground for you as His son or daughter to explore His love, not just "then and there." Dare to believe! Dare to receive! Dare to become! Dare to live like Jesus! *Mesmerize* can ignite His fire of passion and adventure, and you'll never again live a mundane life.

Fred & Pat Bruner
Apostolic Leaders, Hope Church
Builders, Bethel Leaders Network

Mesmerize is a book that beautifully maps out what it is to see and operate on a supernatural level. David Edwards reveals that if Jesus is truly going to receive his full reward, it will come through his body—His family. This book will accelerate you and prepare your ability to think outside of the box. After reading it, I am convinced that God has so much more for us. He is still speaking and doing new things. I believe Dave wrote *Mesmerize* to restore, transform, and equip God's family to see into the heavenly realms for Kingdom Impact.

Chris Oliver
Founder & Senior Pastor, Resurgent ATL Church

Anticipation arises when I know David Edwards has penned yet another book. In doing life with him and his wife, Allessia, we regularly process fresh revelations and encounters. Dave's understanding provokes you to engage The Word, and The Word made flesh—The Person of Jesus. His testimonies cause a curiosity that produces a fruitful outcome of greater revelation, higher truths, and knowledge to apply daily. In *Mesmerize,* he shares moments that are "an open invitation for us to insert ourselves into the stories," building our faith and hope in the more. I believe that as you read, you will be wrapped up in the fabric of Truth Himself. Discover the ability, capacity, and opportunity to explore and behold as sons and daughters of Abba, God. I pray you have eyes to see as "On Earth as it is in Heaven!"

Stephanie McMinn
Founder, Be Generous
Sr. Associate Leader, Awaken Family Church

In his new book, *Mesmerize*, my friend David Edwards brilliantly articulates revelation on what it's like when heaven and earth become one. The revelation that David shares comes from someone who has truly been mesmerized by his God in a place of an intimate relationship, where two become one. Living from this place of oneness with God the Father, God the Son, and God the Holy Spirit is key to living a victorious Christian life. It brings to mind a wonderful revelation that the Godhead is no longer just three in one but four in one, as born-again believers filled with the Holy Spirit are included in His family. Realizing this partnership with the Godhead brings the reality of heaven into our lives. I believe through this book, you will lock eyes with Jesus and be completely mesmerized by Him, experiencing oneness that produces a supernatural life full of signs, wonders, and miracles.

Myles Kilby
Pastor, The River Church
Host, *Your Breakthrough Today*

As I read *Mesmerize*, my heart became more convinced than ever that God is still interacting with His people in mind-blowing, life-transforming ways. Dave's book is an invitation to biblical levels of supernatural encounters through captivating true stories. Your heart will grow in expectation as you read testimonies of the heavenly realm crashing into the earthly realm.

Julie White
Founder, Royal Daughters of the King

Mesmerize, by David Edwards, is an exceptional invitation for each of us to enter into our own otherworldly experiences and be mesmerized by God. The substance caught within these pages does not just create a hunger for more of God but also brings you into the full knowledge that He created you to live beyond settling for average. From page to page, you will awaken an appetite for supernatural encounters. This book is not merely something to read but a journey to embark on.

Kosie van der Merwe
Founder, Rivers of Revival Ministries and
Compassion Care, Cape Town, South Africa

RECOGNITION

Just as in the stories to come, where words fail to capture the indescribable nature of encountering our God in heavenly places, they also fall short in expressing gratitude to those who helped bring this book to you through their time, talent, and treasure.

I dedicate this book to our Awaken Family Church and School of Revivalists families. Allessia and I had a dream and God wrapped your lives around it. We are thankful that we get to do life together in His presence.

Thanks to Allessia Edwards and Julie White for additional edits, feedback, and encouragement.

Thanks to all of the endorsers for taking the time to read the manuscript, and to Shaun Tabatt for the Foreword.

Thanks to the lives of those who's stories are knitted together with mine to form some of the amazing encounters in this book.

Thanks to our spiritual fathers, mothers, mentors, and friends whose guidance and support shape our lives: Leif & Jennifer Hetland, Chris & Terri Oliver, Greg & Nancy Tankersley, Fred & Pat Bruner, Scott & Lacey Thompson, Jeremy & Naomi Connor, Brandon & Lindsey Weaver, Bryan & Mindy Jackson, Jason & Kelsi Murray, Stephanie McMinn, and our parents & families.

There are so many more that I couldn't name one without naming you all.

TABLE OF CONTENTS

FOREWORD

Looking back on my spiritual journey, the idea of me writing a foreword for a book like *Mesmerize* seems rather funny. This Lutheran Church Missouri Synod-raised boy who married a Baptist girl was completely at home in cessationist circles. I was suspect and critical of anything relating to supernatural signs and wonders. However, God had a different plan. Through my work in Christian publishing and media, He thrust me into the deep end of the Spirit-empowered pool, and my life will never be the same.

David and I met through our mutual friend Laura Douglass and quickly discovered we are both passionate about using print and digital media to tell the world about Jesus. All these years later, I am truly honored and delighted to have the opportunity to write the foreword for this book.

As David says in the opening part of the book, we are sons and daughters in a supernatural family. God has written a Kingdom calling and destiny over each of our lives and that is precisely what the enemy has been working overtime to destroy. I believe we are at a crossroads in culture right now where the depth of need for being seen, knowing that we belong, and fully understanding our true Kingdom Identity could not be greater.

Through mainstream culture and media, the enemy has spent many years sowing seeds of doubt about the supernatural worldview of the Bible, replacing it with counterfeit miracles and spiritual experiences that are nothing more than a distraction and misdirection to lead us away from Jesus.

In the pages of *Mesmerize*, you will come face to face with a God who is active in our world today and fully knowable by His sons and daughters. As you experience the many wonderful dreams and encounters recounted in the book and do the activations at the close of each chapter, God will remove the blinders from your eyes and reveal the fullness of who He created you to be. When you finish this book and close the back flap, I am confident that you will be firmly grounded in your Kingdom family identity and ready to walk in the fullness of the divine destiny that your heart has always longed for.

Shaun Tabatt
Publishing Executive, Destiny Image
Co-Author, *Stories of Heaven and the Afterlife*

PREFACE | GOD IS CREATOR

In the beginning, God created the heavens and the earth.[1] God existed before creation, content within Himself as The Father, The Son, and The Holy Spirit. Yet, He longed to share the joy of love within His Triune Being with those who would choose to love Him. So, God, who is One, became two—Creator and creation. Creation came from God, therefore, always longs to return to God.[2]

In the act of creation, we see one being—Adam—become two, Adam and Eve. We also see two spaces—the heavens and the earth. When the Creator created creation, He created them in His image. One entity becoming two. Because of this, creation will always be drawn back to Creator, husband and wife will always be drawn to one another, and heaven and earth will always be drawn together. It's like an invisible magnet set within the fabric of all things. The goal of the Creator is for all creation to be one, big, happy family—sons and daughters, mothers and fathers, doing life together in God's presence.

This pattern is the design initiated in the beginning, the design restored in Jesus, and the purpose that will complete in the end. The bible says, "all creation longs for the sons and daughters of God to be revealed" because they are the keepers of the design. The Creator is

---

[1] Genesis 1:1
[2] Romans 8:19

revealed to creation in them—and in them, heaven touches earth as family solidifies in the people. This pattern was the Father's happy choice. He set it up this way to reveal Himself to us in a way that we would fall in love with Him and share that love with others. Jesus, the only "begotten" Son, is the key to this plan. He chose to become the Ultimate Act of the Father's love by giving His life for us. In Him, we see the Father's loving nature. A price the Son paid gladly because of the "joy set before Him"—restoring the family to the design and image of the Father.[3]

Sons and daughters who know their identity and place in the Father through the Son, and in the power of the Holy Spirit, are a supernatural family. They expand His kingdom all across creation—filling the void in the hearts of men and even in the fabric of all created things. This kingdom family will, by default, walk in the same signs, wonders, and miracles set before them by their King, Jesus. They will walk in the same manner as the ones who knew God in the bible, performing identical exploits and even exceeding them. This is why the biblical authors recorded the story of God—showing who God is, who His people are, His redemptive plan, and inviting us into our own otherworldly experience with Him.

If we are not supernatural, we are not accessing the fulness of everything that God has for us. Therefore, my heart in writing this book is to share with you how we can be a supernatural family through testimonies, stories, and biblical references. As sons and daughters, we walk

____

[3] Hebrews 12:2

with our Creator, knowing our place in Heaven and Earth.

Miracles and Kingdom Family

The first book in this series, *Mystify*, was primarily a chronology of a series of encounters showing how the elements of creation respond to the revealing and activation of kingdom family. These elements—earth, wind, water, and fire—are always present, manifesting in an array when the presence of God shows up profoundly. This is evident in the bible and throughout church history. Often, it's known as *apocalyptic literature.* It gives the viewpoint of when someone steps from heaven into earth, outside the laws of physics and time, to see the two realms from God's perspective. This can be macro in nature, as we see in Daniel, Ezekiel, and Revelation. It can also be micro in nature, as we read about in some of the Psalms, Elijah in the cave, or Paul's third-heaven trip.

Heaven touching earth and the elements of the earth responding are part of the pattern. The earth is absolutely affected when it's touched by the Creator. Because this is the design, natural elements will react to supernatural input. The fallen one, Lucifer, who was the first orphan, rebelling against God's design and stepping out of His image and family, knows this. He knows that God is supernatural and that His people are supernatural. He also knows that the design of creation is for God's people to have interaction in heaven and on earth. Therefore, his goal is to pervert the plan, the expression of the supernatural, and unleash hell on earth.

Heaven on earth is always redemptive.

Hell on earth is always destructive.

Each will be known by the fruit it bears. If it brings life abundantly, its origin is Jesus—the Restorer of the Plan, Repairer of the Breach.[4] If it steals, kills, and destroys, then it's a perversion from the fallen one—the accuser and slanderer.[5] If you're unsure of the origin, follow the fruit: did it create or pervert?

Jesus in you is the plumbline, validated by His word. Supernatural power that perverts, impersonates, or directly opposes God's plan is still supernatural power, but of a lower order. The space between heaven and earth is known as the second heaven. This space is where the enemy resides. He was depowered, defeated, and humiliated by Jesus on the cross.[6] Jesus' life in us removes the stain of the enemy's fallen influence. Satan doesn't want us to know this. He doesn't want us to understand our heavenly seat or place in kingdom family.[7] And he will do anything to stop it. He will call supernatural power that flows from the third heaven to earth evil, false, and heretical.[8] He always falsely labels identity in the natural and heavenly families. Natural

---

[4] Isaiah 58:12 – Jesus is the answered prayer, the answered fast, the One standing between (and therefore connecting) heaven and earth. In Him, the distance between heaven and earth is narrowed and erased. In contrast, the enemy's goal is to widen the gap and cause us to remain orphans, disconnected from the Father, His Family, and everything we inherit through His Son (Ephesians 1:14).

[5] John 10:10

[6] Colossians 2:11-15

[7] Ephesians 2:6

[8] Luke 11:15 (read whole chapter for context). Jesus reveals the Lord's prayer, wherein heaven flows to earth, which includes the casting out of demons. The response of the enemy was to misidentify and invalidate the miracle. Satan always responds this way when the Kingdom of Heaven invades, disempowers, and evicts the kingdom of darkness.

and heavenly power and family are known by love.[9] Love can only flow from above. Satan has no love, only fear, lies, and deceit. He uses these as weapons to convince God's family that anything supernatural is from his realm, not the Father's. The last thing he wants is for us to know our identity[10] as sons and daughters who reign from heaven to earth, defeating his remaining influence and accelerating God's plan.

The second heaven can manipulate the elements, fake miracles, and empower false religions. But just as Aaron's serpent ate the serpents of Pharaoh, which was symbolic of Yahweh defeating the gods of Egypt, true miracles that flow from heaven to earth will always expose the false.[11] In reality, the truth cannot be known without demonstration. Speaking the word releases the voice of Jesus to cut down the enemy's plans while simultaneously redeeming God's plan. His word is power. His signs, wonders, and miracles reveal His true nature, cancel the enemy's assignment, and reveal kingdom family.

If the enemy cannot deceive us with false miracles, his backup plan is to try to convince us that all miracles are false. Everything Jesus did was to empower us in everything He calls us to do. When we are doing Jesus things—signs, wonders, and miracles—we reveal Jesus. We show who Jesus is to the ones who need to know Him. They don't need a powerless, non-supernatural speech

---

[9] John 13:35

[10] See Genesis 3:1- The enemy's question, "Has God said?" What God says to us is the anchor of our identity. Satan's scheme is to question our relationship with God, causing us to doubt who the Father says we are as His sons and daughters.

[11] Exodus 7:8-13

about Him. They need Him as He is, full of supernatural power, love, and wisdom.[12] They need a gospel, theology, and witness that looks like Jesus. When we look like Jesus, they will know we are members of His family, and their internal design will activate, drawing them back to Creator as they find their place in His family.

Mystify Series

The Hebraic concept of time spirals upwards and expands. It's not the same chronological system we use today. With each rising and expanding circle in the spiral, some previous events are revisited in a broadened way. The story is viewed and expanded like looking through layers of lenses that focus on different points.

Mystify was written in story form to show what happens when sons and daughters walk in their identity. Identity and family are the layers set for us to continue the story in *Mesmerize*. Don't worry; if you begin here, the story will stand on its own. You'll be able to read *Mystify* with *Mesmerize* as a base. Book One was about the earthly realm responding to the heavenly realm. Our goal here will reverse the angle. Book Two will be about experiencing the heavenly realms and seeing encounters in the earth from that perspective.

As you read, keep a listening ear for Holy Spirit to speak to you. My goal is for you to hear clearer and see better everything God is showing you and speaking to you. I pray that as you read the pages to come, you are mesmerized by the glory of God and experience Him in ever-increasing ways!

---

[12] 2 Timothy 1:7

CHAPTER 1 | ANGEL SOUNDS

"Where's the helicopter?"

"Huh? Ah, There's no helicopter here!"

"Didn't a helicopter just fly overhead? We heard the sound."

"Nope."

Perplexed, they went back into the old church.

Focusing back on worship, curious wonder fluttered in their imagination. Of all the glory they would experience that night, it wouldn't be until the next day that they would realize that the sounds that invaded the church were not that of a helicopter but of angels.

What Does it Sound like When Heaven Comes Down?

In my first book, *The Call for Revivalists*, I posed a question from a popular worship song, "What does it look like when heaven comes down?" Here, I pose a similar question, "What does it sound like when heaven comes down?"

The answer is as endless as music.

Each moment from Him—from heaven to earth—will continually transform the earth with wonder. Wonder, after all, is the state from which we were created and from which we create. When found in wonder, we come alive, flourishing in the everlasting dreams the Creator paints over our lives.

Encounters are moments of wonder, moments of music. In God's design, they create. When we encounter God, He creates something new in us. We become part of His song. He continues to sing through us as we create. His sound animates our lives, inspiring others through the frequency our heart sings.

In *The Magician's Nephew*, CS Lewis's masterful allegory of creation, Aslan, who represents God, sings the imaginary universe of Narnia into existence.

> In the darkness, something was happening at last. A voice had begun to sing... the blackness overhead, all at once, was blazing with stars. They didn't come out gently one by one as on a summer evening. One moment there had been nothing but darkness; next moment a thousand, thousand points of light leaped out.[13]

Genesis tells us that in the beginning, God created the world through His word. The Apostle, John, extends this by revealing God's word is alive. The word with Him,

---

[13] C.S. Lewis, *The Magician's Nephew* (New York: Collier, 1955), p. 98-99.

in the beginning, was Jesus. Jesus, the Living Word, is the sound of creation emanating from the Father and animating all life in our universe (John 1:1-5).

His songs are all around us. Creation is His medley. The beauty of Jesus is that He is the note from Papa's heart. When He came, He restored creation's sound to His Father's frequency. Jesus shows us how to recognize His sound in us and creation. We become His tuning fork, harmonizing creation back to Himself.

David, the Psalmist who transformed atmospheres through worship, revealed the power that the sound of God has when released in the earth. The atmosphere within David became the atmosphere around David as creation harmonized with Creator. God is lovesick for those who are lovesick for Him. I believe that as God heard the sound of David's heart echoing across the earth, their hearts synchronized.

Creator and creation—Father and Son.

The prophet Isaiah described this connection as "The Key of David" (Is 22:22). Through lovesick worship, David found the keys that unlock doors no one can open—heavenly doors, the very heart of God. He was love-drenched by His King. The King's heart is captured through worship. Worship is the heart of nobility that empowers heavenly access and kingship in the earth. A man or woman after God's own heart will unlock His song and produce the sound of heaven on earth. Jesus later reveals that the church is to operate in this vein (Mt 16).

What does it sound like when heaven comes down or when earth goes up? Call and recall? Earth sounding like heaven? I believe that is God's desire and the secret to worship. When His world invades ours, our world will begin to sound like His.

Angel Mix Tape

"Follow me!"

With eyes of fire and a heart of flames, Jaxon marched with intensity towards his room. Chris, Avi, and I were in tow. He grabbed his tape recorder as he entered, swung around, and pressed play. Yes, CDs had been around for nearly twenty years by then, but cassette tapes were cheap, readily available, and often used in churches to record ministry, worship, and prophetic words.

Prior to this, we had heard about a worship service that had a recording of angels singing and that someone even had a copy of it. Before YouTube and MP3, hardcopy was how encounters were shared. Even the Brownville Revival didn't go viral online. Instead, it spread via VHSs as VCRs became portals of heavenly glory.

Back when I was in youth group, we would drive to watch the latest tape someone brought back from the Brownsville Revival to experience a fresh touch of God. It was beautiful in a way. However, it required planning and pursuit to capture the latest revival moment. I love that today's technology allows us to see and share what God is doing instantly, but it has its downsides. We can easily dismiss it, judge it, and even disbelieve it. Using wisdom and discernment are necessary, but this approach has caused many to use their heads to shut down their hearts, preventing them from receiving a fresh touch from God. It was this pursuit that led me to Jaxon and the heavenly moment captured on a cassette.

Hot Florida air blows gently from the oscillating fan in front of the open window as we stare at the little grey box.

"What is this?" we ask.

"You'll see!" he says with a slight smirk and squinting, as if he is setting us up for something.

Static sounds, the spinning of tape, and slight voices begin to rise. After a few seconds of warped playback, worship burst through the small, way too trebly, speaker.

"Is this what I think it is," I ask intently.

"Just wait, you'll hear it kick in," he grins.

Even though we were all students at Brownsville Revival School of Ministry and in the middle of one of the greatest revivals the world had ever seen, we were not content with stopping there. The revival environment demanded, rather, beckoned us into more and more of God. We were hungry and burning, with hearts throbbing to experience God in every way possible. We lived our lives in a constant state of expectation. Our daily convos centered around what God did yesterday, what God would do today, and excitement for what tomorrow would bring. We were on the hunt for His presence. God was all around us, but all we wanted was more of God.

Stories of revival, encounters, and other moves of the Spirit from were rich in the chatter of the student body. This is how our group of friends heard about a recording of angels singing. Jaxon did some digging and found that it wasn't just glory gossip, but that one of the students actually had a copy of it…or a copy of a copy, which he, of course, copied.

As the gears turned, we tuned our hearts to the worship emanating from the hard-working speaker. It was a fiery set. They were passionately singing and making heavenly declarations. Their voices were few but powerful. You could tell this was a small group of saints simply going after Jesus. There were maybe a couple of male and female singers, a guitar, keys, and percussion of some type. A few background vocals could be heard singing along and declaring. You could also hear the spaces in the air that would have been filled with other instruments if they were available. Awkward gaps replaced sections of filler as they pressed on.

We were about three minutes into the track when suddenly, those gaps began to fade. The notes sounded fuller. Either the bassist was late, or one from another realm joined in. The background voices began to fill the room when they sounded scattered at best only seconds before. It took a moment for those leading the set to realize what was happening. Then, excitement burst through as they were both eager to continue and stunned by the sudden visitation.

Next, angelic voices began to harmonize with theirs. It was as if their voices energized the voices of the singers. Heaven and earth sang together.

Our faces became too weak for our jaws as they dropped to the floor. Jaxon soaked up our reaction. I probably said something like, "Whoa, wait, what, wow, is that? I hear it!"

Gravity recovered grins now shined as we exchanged glances in the dimly lit room filled with heavenly sounds.

We were in the same house I mentioned in *Mystify*, where Jaxon and Avi had the Jesus encounter. Expectation and intimacy with God set the atmosphere for our home to be full of glory. That is all we wanted, day and night. It both made me who I am today and kept me loyal to the heart of God. I could fill the entire book with encounters just from our time living next to the BRSM campus at Bay Pine Villas.

A hum gradually filled the air in conjunction with the angelic sounds. Was it wind, vibration, both? As uncommon as this encounter seems, wind and vibrations often accompany them. The plus side of modern technology is that we now have access to more and more of these experiences with better capture quality. Their stories fill both the bible and church history, and now we can record and share them like never before.

With the hum came a greater intensity. The human voices faded as angelic tones rose. Giggles of joy became silent as the majesty filled the room.

After a crescendo of power, as if there were thousands in attendance with every type of angelic instrument—an orchestra of many waters—they quickly phased out, leaving only whispers and crackles from the human voices. Jaxon stops the tape as we embrace a moment of recovery.

Times like these are a recipe for glory. My journey in the Lord went from ministry school student to ministry school director. And I often tell my students that God fills our deficits, whether it's love, family, finances, or any place that feels empty. We must realize that He supplies everything we need, everything we lack, and everything we long for. He also adds to spaces that are full and transforms them to overflow.

Spontaneous Invasion

One of the most well-known encounters like this is from the ministry of Dr. Rodney Howard-Browne. I will not dive into all the details as it is readily available from his ministry and on YouTube.[14] But I do include it because it is another step in my journey of experiencing the angelic. However, I may need to retrace my steps because we can have encounters such as these and not even know it. The bible says that many have entertained angels unaware (Heb 13:2). Hopefully, both you and I will become more aware by stewarding our encounters and having hearts of expectation for more.

Dr. Howard-Browne is the grandfather of revival in our generation. He was one of the first to experience fresh outbreaks of holy laughter. His ministry influenced the Toronto Blessing and the Brownsville Revival in Pensacola, FL.

The encounter I am referring to is known as The Sound of Angels. This recording was a step up from the previous story because they captured it on video. Expectation was rich at his meetings. This meeting happened in the early 1990s, and the hearts of the thousands in attendance were primed for revival.

---

14 Rodney Howard-Browne, *The Realms of God*, January 1994: https://youtu.be/TqTC1qVuNCE (scan qr code)

After worship, Rodney went up to simply take the offering. As he read a passage of Scripture, he became heavy from the weighty glory filling the room, and his speech began to slur. The people recognized that God's presence was invading and began to respond with laughs, giggles, and excitement. Some sat in silence while others ran around the room. Those overcome by the Holy Spirit even started falling out in their pews as more stood and danced.

He began to worship and coach them through the moment exclaiming "holy, holy," along with other declarations. Others followed this spiritual momentum as a melodic yet spontaneous song filled the auditorium.

After a few minutes, a higher octave sound joined in. It was subtle at first but soon could be heard by crowds of people. With the previous experience, we could only listen to what was happening. Here, I observed the people's response to the chorus of angels singing with them. Many went Holy Ghost "bananas." Shouts, groans, cries, and manifestations broke out as heaven broke in.

The angelic singing sounded as if it was riding above the voices of the people. It was beautiful beyond words. My heart began to burn not just to experience this via a recording but to hear it in real-time.

"Celestial Odyssey"

Another step in my journey came when I first heard "Celestial Odyssey," a ballad[15] recalling the apocalyptic voyage to heaven of singer, Freddy Hayler. He recalls

---

15 Freddy Hayler, *The Celestial Odyssey*:
https://youtu.be/mgFpKi4hSoQ (scan qr code)

"angelic beings singing beautiful songs" as they encompassed God's throne in his vision. Like the Apostle John, who shared the experiences with angels in his apocalypse (the Book of Revelation), Freddy's voyage was highlighted by seeing Jesus and the Father on His throne. Angels have one goal, which is to guide us to Jesus. Any angelic encounter has this in mind.

God allows us to gaze upon Him and all that surrounds Him within the heavenly family. His desire is for the families of heaven and earth to be one. When we have encounters like this, He reveals His nature to us in our walk, gives us a testimony to share with others what the heavenly realm is like, and transforms the earth to mirror heaven.

What does it look like, sound, and feel like when heaven comes down? It looks like Jesus, it looks like us, and it looks like family. If His throne is near, what we experience will sound like His throne—full of fire, wind, vibration, water, angelic beings, thundering, lightning, and so much more. Vocabulary falls far short of definition. When we experience heavenly encounters, we experience Jesus. We become more like Him.

When Sid Roth interviewed me for his show, It's Supernatural,[16] he asked me this question, "Why did you write *Mystify*?" My response was simple: "When I read the bible, it's an invitation for me to insert myself into the story and experience God the same way the heroes of the faith did. So, when I began to have my own encounters, I wanted to share them so they can experience Him in all

---

[16] Sid Roth, *It's Supernatural,* guest, David Edwards: https://youtu.be/A2oMIRN5ubw (scan qr code)

the ways He's made Himself available." God's kids experiencing God is heaven on earth. It's glorious!

Heaven in LaSalle

Near the end of 2019, Allessia and I were invited to speak at an event in LaSalle, IL, by our dear friend, Shay Arthur. She is the leader of the ministry, Ignite A Movement. We went with her close friend, Jessica, on a trip to Cuba that year and were looking forward to a reunion with her and other team members in Illinois. Our hearts believed God for a fresh touch as we were carrying momentum from witnessing unique manifestations on the mission field.

After a sketchy landing at Chicago Midway Airport, we met up with Jed, another Cuba team member. Then we hopped in our rental car and headed west. Along the way, we caught up, reminiscing about Havana, and set our sights on everything we felt God wanted to do. But we weren't quite prepared for what was to come. God has a way of exceeding our expectations.

Upon arrival, we rendezvoused for some lunch with the rest of the group, covering logistics for the evening meeting. I was busy vlogging our adventure so we could share all that God had on his heart with our YouTube channel[17] (Link below, go check it out and subscribe for extra content!).

Alex Guthrie and Heidi Williams of Haven House Worship led worship that night. Even during rehearsal, the presence of God was rich. I talked with Jessica and

---

[17] The Sound of Angels: https://youtu.be/ilgzGsnPOXc (scan qr code)

others about how much glory was already there. The church building that Abundant Life Fellowship meets at is old. Several different churches have called it home since it's construction. Ornate brick covers the facade with an architectural roof line. Stained glass inspires the onlooker from both inside and out. There were several ridges of varying height with a bell tower near the entryway.

The sanctuary inside had charming arches of varying diameters with round white pillars gently carrying their weight. The front of the space is where old meets new, as a makeshift wall was in place to separate the kid's area. Above the balcony was a large brass pipe organ. The Indiana Jones in me went to check it out, finding it partially disassembled and inaccessible. Above it loomed the bell tower, which I climbed up as far as I could before a locked trap door ended my ascent.

From my perched position, I looked down at the pews below and thought about all the lives touched here through different ministries and expressions. How many were saved, healed, delivered, and restored? How many stories could these bricks and pillars tell about Papa touching His kids in this place? Legacy prophesies destiny. Encounters can be pioneered but in a space like this, I believe we tapped into a well of revival.

We had no more than begun with only a small group of us gathered when Alex and Heidi began to sing Bethel Music's song, Angels:

Calling all angels,
Calling the watchmen angels on the walls

To come and sing with us.[18]

Having vlogged a good portion of the day, I took a break from recording to focus on the Lord as we plunged into the depths of His heart. As they sang, their voices echoed in the natural acoustics of the over 100-year-old walls. The sound it created was mesmerizing. You could feel the old church come to life as heaven seemed to join in. Adoration.

A sound.

Another.

"Whomp, Whomp, Whomp"

There are normal sounds that linger in the background of whatever you're doing. Our brains subconsciously cancel most of them out. But sometimes they break through.

I didn't pay much attention at first as the sound entered the atmosphere. It seemed to stall a bit. It took a second for me to realize I was hearing something else as I was so engaged in worship. When the sound continued, my mind fed me a natural explanation for what was happening.

Jake break?

Next, I went from glorious worship to annoyance. Finding a natural conclusion for the sound I heard, my heart became upset because I thought a semitruck was slowly driving passed the church applying its engine break. Although, it still didn't make sense. Engine breaks

---

[18] © 2011 Bethel Music Publishing (ASCAP). All rights reserved. Used by permission.

("Jake Breaks") are used when decelerating and wouldn't generate such a prolonged noise.

At the time, it didn't really phase me. I am not sure how long it lasted, but I found myself back in worship as the noise faded. I had no idea the depth of what had just occurred or that anyone else heard it or, much less, investigated it.

Simultaneously to my experience, Shay and another friend, Rachel, bolted out of the church, down the small set of stairs and onto the sidewalk, they ran over to some people walking by and asked, "Where's the helicopter?"

Hearing the "Whomp, Whomp, Whomp," they assumed a helicopter was landing nearby the building. Yet, when they surveyed the sky, it was absent of all flying contraptions.

"Huh?" met with confused gazes at the audacity of the question. LaSalle is an hour outside Chicago, past the outer edge of suburbia. It sits in a cluster of small towns. It would be a rare sight indeed to see a helicopter flying through the city. Any jets would still be too high to make an impact.

"Uh, no helicopters here!" they answered with raised eyebrows as they continued up the street, perhaps walking slightly quicker than before.

The girls wondered where the sound came from as they wandered back inside to reengage in worship.

Others had similar experiences. They all heard it. Some thought a train was going by at the tracks down by the river. Allessia's dad was a train engineer for over 30 years, so we knew it wasn't that, but we would later discover that all of us heard the sound and assumed it came from something natural outside. But deep down, our spirits knew. The sound filled the room; it didn't originate outside but above.

As the evening continued, we transitioned from worship with several sharing their heart. A few more people showed up as Allessia, and I got up to speak about revival. I talked about the fires of God flowing from generation to generation and moving across the globe. I highlighted the Hebrides Revival in Scotland, where they prayed Psalm 24 and asked:

"God, are my hands clean? Is my heart pure?"

My bride then told the story of Pastor John Kilpatrick crying out to God all alone in the middle of the night at Brownsville Assembly, proclaiming:

"God there's more, there's got to be MORE!"

These prayers stained history. These prayers were answered. God showed up in the Hebrides as the presence of God fell on the community in such a powerful way, those sleeping woke up and ran to the church, "gripped by the awareness of God." God showed up at Brownsville, sparking a five-year revival that saw between 250k – two million souls come into the kingdom and touch over five million lives.

People came to the altar to grab hold of God as we spoke. Heidi began to sing the songs flowing through her heart. We waited and connected. His presence was so heavy that some could barely move. Others were getting touched and healed. Many signs and wonders occurred.

Some even testified about a vision they saw or a miracle they received.

At one point near the end, I looked up and noticed that a glory cloud had filled the area where the pipe organ was housed. I pointed it to Shay as others began to see it. For many, it was the first time they saw His glory. The whole ceiling was hazy, but it was the most concentrated around the organ. It appeared as a light mist. We could still see the pipes, but their shimmer was distorted by the Shekinah that held it tight. This was answered cry for some as they came hoping to see God in a tangible way.

The night was "altogether lovely." Heaven's "sloppy wet kiss" was to gift us with a multisensory encounter enveloped in His presence.

The next day we met as a team to debrief and prepare for that evening's service at the coffee shop with our friend Alex sharing Jesus with the broader community. During our talk, we discovered that we had all heard the sound. We knew what our hearts had already been telling us. We had experienced an angelic visitation.

The "Whomp, Whomp, Whomp" wasn't a semi-truck, train, or even helicopter. Although, I joked, "It could've been helicopter angels."[19] Delight filled the room as our faces could not refrain from skin-stretching smiles. We had experienced a supernatural manifestation together. It created a bond between us, a recognition that we all knew that heaven had touched us and that the sound was real, evident, and acknowledged by us all.

---

[19] Interestingly, "helicopter" means spiral wing. Many Hebraic depictions of Cherubim and the Four Living Creatures seem to have a spiral shape. Could they sound like a helicopter?

Other stories describe the sound of heavenly beings similarly flapping their wings. In the Book of Acts, the sound of the wind of the Spirit filled the house where they were sitting. In Andrew Murray's South African prayer meetings, they heard a heavenly sound way off in the distance get louder and louder until it filled the meeting place.

Even though I had turned off my video camera, we found out several weeks later that someone had recorded the audio from the night. Alex sent me the file, which did indeed capture the sound. You can't make out the distinct "Whomp' sounds, but you can hear the hum as it enters the building and slowly becomes louder before fading out. It sounds like a swirling wind.

Along with the sound from the night, he also sent another recording from twenty years ago of a similar encounter in northern Canada. A native tribe had gathered to pray for the youth in their community. The clip was from the Sentinel Group's "Transformations Three" documentary. You can hear them worshipping and praying as the sound gradually fills the room until it's almost overwhelming. The people responded in a holy chorus full of wonder, cries, and shouts of "fire, fire!" Witnesses said, "things started to shake, people started to shake." "It sounded like a jet," but just like there were no helicopters in LaSalle, there were no jets that far north in Canada (you can watch it in the link provided in footnote 17).

Check out the vlog from the trip in the link below.[20] I pray that in adding these links, your experience with this book will be enhanced as you not only get to read about many of the amazing stories, but you'll also get to watch highlights, making it a multi-sensory journey!

Activation

1. Think about moments you have had in the past that may have been written off as natural. Ask Holy Spirit if there was more than meets the eye. Journal what He shows you and ask God to both take you back into that experience and give you a new one.
2. In worship moments this week, whether by yourself or in a corporate gathering, look, listen, and feel the atmosphere. Small noticeable differences are often the gateway to extravagant encounters in His presence.

---

[20] LaSalle Vlog: https://youtu.be/RwwEpJNwFnE
(Scan qr code)

CHAPTER 2 | THE PORCH

I looked over the edge of the porch to see if Jesus was in the yard. Our conversation had just been interrupted by so much glory we thought we might see Him as we extraordinarily felt His presence. It was the middle of the night, but that didn't stop creatures all around us from noticing too, even singing their praises! Geese at the lake down the street cried out, "honk, honk," as they scrambled into the air at heaven's sudden manifestation.

The Wild Goose

In Wales and other Celtic lands, Holy Spirit is often called "The Wild Goose" because it symbolizes God's nature when He is moving unpredictably. Wales is known as "The Land of Revival" as they have experienced multiple revivals on a national level. True revival cannot be contained. I've found something in the hearts of the Celtic saints that resolves to let the Wild Goose loose. Revival fires can ignite on various levels, but the heart must be willing to let the whole thing burn to get to the point where the entire country is impacted. Revivalists such as Evan Roberts and Duncan Campbell found themselves in detonated revivals and were disinclined to clip the wings of the wild goose.

The prophetic voices of Bob Jones, Justin Abraham, and others have shared words about the wild goose flying freely in our generation. Creation—birds and animals, the stars and the sky—are often prophetic pictures of what God is doing. Recognizing how God speaks through them is key to understanding His heart and plan for us.

Jesus uses imagery from creation to reveal how to recognize the times:

> One day some of the Pharisees and those of the Jewish sect known as the Sadducees approached Jesus, insisting that he prove to them that he was the Messiah. "Show us a supernatural sign from heaven," they demanded.
>
> Jesus answered, "You can read the signs of the weather, for you say, 'Red sky at night, sailors delight.' And, 'Red sky in the morning, sailors take warning.' You're so adept at forecasting the weather by looking at the sky, but you're absolutely clueless in reading the obvious signs of the times. A wicked and wayward generation always asks for signs, but the only sign I provide for you will be the sign of Jonah the prophet." Then he turned away and left them.
>
> ~Matthew 16:1-4 TPT

Jesus performed signs all around them. When they questioned Him, asking for a sign—to prove Himself in a manner that fit in their box. Could Jesus do something apocalyptic in front of them (a form of submitting to their authority) to prove to them (or gain their acceptance) that He was Messiah? The validity of whether or not "signs" were from God was not the question; rather, it was whether Jesus would stop being a wild goose and adjust His ministry to their demands.

After my "Sid Roth's It's Supernatural" episode aired, a small number of viewers called into question the validity of the miraculous testimonies from *Mystify*. One of the verses used in their argument was the one above, specifically: "A wicked and wayward generation always asks for signs, but the only sign I provide for you will be the sign of Jonah the prophet." Jesus, Himself said this to Pharisees asking for a sign when Jesus was already performing many signs and wonders. Jesus would, in no way, turn to His accusers and proclaim that "signs" in themselves were "wicked." Instead, His rebuke was that they were "absolutely clueless in reading the obvious signs of the times." Because the Pharisees weren't accurately interpreting the times, they failed to recognize Jesus as Messiah. Jesus responds by showing them the signs themselves were signs of the times. If they looked at scripture the same way they perceived weather patterns, they would've identified Jesus accurately, knowing that His signs and wonders were from the Father.

Sadly, this pattern continues today. It's a pattern that misidentifies Jesus and revival, believing that "signs" are "wicked." On the contrary, looking for a sign outside of a relationship with Jesus is wicked. Questioning the signs of Jesus is wicked. Demanding a sign when signs are already present is wicked. Jesus didn't have to prove Himself then, and He doesn't have to prove Himself now. Jesus, Himself, is the Sign—Who entered the earth and, like Jonah, emerged three days later. Let us not misidentify Jesus moving among us. He is the Revelation, the way, the truth, and the life.[21]

The natural realm—the earth and sky, harmonize with Jesus' appearance. His footsteps on the earth cause it to rumble with joy. His breath in the air causes the sky to sing. Like the Sons of Issachar,[22] if we can see the effects of His presence, we will recognize when He is near. We will "understand the times and know what we should do." He will be with us, and the signs that followed Him will follow us. So likewise, creation will react to us the same way it responded to Him.

One night, in the great city of Tyrone, GA, my good friend, Scott Thompson, and I found ourselves in this exact place. We were sitting on his porch, briars in hand, as we tapped into our inner "Inklings" as JRR Tolkien and CS Lewis often did at the Eagle and Child pub in Oxford, England. When, seemingly in response to our conversation, creation around us began to cry out as God's presence moved over the neighborhood like a fog rolling in.

A Family Reigning from Heaven to Earth

Humans are created in God's image. As such, they are His *imagers*[23] in creation. When humans reign with

---

[21] John 14:6

[22] Read 1 Chronicles 12 (specifically vs 32) for context.

[23] One who images or forms likeness.

Jesus in heavenly places, creation responds to the rule of this heavenly family.

A Bird's Eye View

What if you're a bird? What would it be like to be able to fly to wherever you need to go? What goes through your mind? What is a bird's worldview? Are birds aware of their Creator and their place in His creation? Is there something inside creation itself that pings when His family is present? Is it part of their instinct or DNA?

We know that the pattern of creation is family. Basic deduction would conclude that creation doesn't operate at its fullest unless this family is ruling. We know from Scripture that the Older Brother[24] of this family, Jesus, restored their rule. Now, they have a great commission to cover all creation with this rule, the same given in the garden. The Older Brother is the King of this Kingdom, and the Gospel of this Kingdom is the mission of this family. Wherever this family is present, the King is present because His presence lives within them.

If you're a bird, do you know when God is present, when His sons and daughters are present? Birds are creations from a Creator, so do they come fully alive when His imagers rule and reign with His Son? If you're a bird, are you like, "Wait a sec, something's happening, YES! the King is near." Then you start birding harder than you've ever birded before?

I know this is a bit silly, but I think this is how a child would think about being a bird. And if birds know

---

24 Romans 8:26, Hebrews 2:11

when His presence is present, I think they would react, cry out, and rejoice in both the coming and the nearness of the King. *Mystify* was full of stories like this, creation—elements, animals, people, all responding to the Father and His family. Creation can only become everything that it was intended to be when we realize our identity and place in His family.

A Conversation

That little detour about the paradigm of creation was designed to set you up for my conversation with Scott. Hopefully, it prepares you for what's to come when we, as sons of God, begin to talk about God, which initiated a response from creation. Now back to that Tyrone night...

Our wives went to a painting class with friends that evening, leaving Scott and me to engage in gentlemen's activities. The revelation that men and women rule and reign coequally with Christ doesn't eliminate the way they were created and their natural need to have time with one another. In fact, the misunderstanding of this has led to unnatural expressions. Healthy heavenly family is revealed when sons and daughters, husbands and wives, know their identity within the Creator. Family cannot be revealed through misidentifying oneself. Only when we see God as He is will we see ourselves as He sees us. This perspective will ignite our identity in Him, completing the circle of Creator and Creation, as revealed through husbands and wives. If it abandons this model, it is no longer an accurate representation of His image. His majestic love covers all, luring our hearts to the fulness of His image. When healthy family is present, it reveals to creation who He really is and who they are.

As such, I need "man" time and Allessia needs "lady" time. This makes me feel manly, and her feel womanly. We can tap into and express that part of ourselves in ways that we cannot with members of the opposite sex. So, as our wives went out to do feminine things, we entered the realm of masculinity. Accompanied by a sip of goodness and a tinge of sophistication, our conversation ensued.

Scott and I were workout partners for years and were so at the time, trading imaginary badges of honor about the pain we felt from the soreness of a recent WOD. Next, we discussed the "rut" as it was that time of year. However, you may give me a demerit on my man card for this, but Scott was the only hunter present in the conversation, although am sure I'll find myself in the woods with him at some point. Continuing, we moved past the need to bond as men in the natural as our need to bond as brothers in the spirit took over.

When Earth Goes to Heaven

Scott's house at the time was a modern version of a country home. It had a grand porch wrapped from the front left around the right side. A walkway led from the street to a wide staircase that ascended to the front door. Large bushes nestled right up to the lattice underneath. A gentle slope rose in the yard from the front to the back of the house, where it met at ground level.

We sat on the right side of the house, overlooking one of the bushes and several trees in his yard. The sun had been at rest for quite some time as our hearts turned to things above. We quickly realized we were both burdened for more of the Lord. Our quest was Jesus. If you've read any of my other books, I often remark that Jesus loves to listen in on those who are talking about Him. We see this when the two disciples lost in conversation on the road to Emmaus became found by Jesus, as you will read about in a coming chapter.

Our awareness of His presence began to rise like a thermometer in boiling water. Mercury shot towards the 100s as we felt Him all around us.

We reminisced about different moves of God we experienced together as it charged our hunger for more. The more we talked, the more our spiritual senses heightened. As the night cooled, our hearts heated up.

We both were part of the extended family from Bethel Church in Redding, CA. Bill Johnson's book, *When Heaven Invades Earth*, not only impacted us but has become part of our worldview and culture. We believe it is heaven's desire and design to fill the earth. We have access to all of heaven and all of God. But even in apprehending this, we still discover new questions in the mystery and are always looking for "more."

"What does it look like when "more" of heaven comes down?" By asking the question again, we opened up the other senses: "What does it sound like? What does it feel like?" What happens when we are fully engulfed by heaven—body, mind, and spirit? What happens on earth when there is a man or woman fully possessed by God?

The angelic encounter of the previous chapter happened several years after this. I didn't notice the connection between them until now.

Sound.

By experiencing Heaven touch earth, we groan for heaven to again touch earth more powerfully. This shift causes us to consider God moving in ways we beforehand either overlooked or were oblivious to. God doesn't stop moving. He may do it again, but there is always the seed of the "more" hidden within. He calls us to step out into the mystery and explore more of Him. Having all of Jesus makes you want more of Jesus. If I see Him, I want to hear Him. If I hear Him, I want to feel Him.

In one of our workouts earlier that week, the movie "Close Encounters of the Third Kind" became the talk in-between lifts. We had both watched the movie's climax and were surprised at the coincidence. Only, we soon found out it was "Jehovah Sneaky" setting us up for more.

After several UFO sightings and dozens of people abducted by aliens over the years, the scientists in the film were trying to figure out a way to communicate with them. They eventually discover the answer to be sound. So, they set up a place in the desert and played specific notes they thought the aliens would respond to. Suddenly, a spaceship appeared and played the notes back.

The movie enhanced our perception of the various ways God chooses to communicate to us. We then compared the interaction with the aliens in the movie to having a heavenly encounter.

"What does an encounter sound like? Are their heavenly notes playing from our spirits to God and back again?"

As I always do, I got excited and compared what we were dreaming about to the Hebrides Revival in Scotland, where a portal opened up between heaven and earth, just like in "Marvel's The Avengers."[25] The people could see into heaven with all the wonder and majesty peering through. This gave us a mental picture to expand our questions into the endless realm of the more of God.

We gazed out into the blackness of night. The light from his house met with shadow on his lawn with a couple of distant streetlamps winking at us between swaying tree limbs. A soft orange glow hovered above the tree line from the surrounding neighbors. Scattered stars peeked through a light layer of cirrus clouds. Our discussion was a mixture of conversive contemplation. With frequent pauses we found that the more we talked, the less we needed to as our spirits communicated what our mouths could not.

A starlit smile shoots across Scott's face as he looks me straight in the eyes and asks, "What would it look like for earth to go to heaven? What if, instead of asking for heaven to come earth, earth went to heaven?"

"What would..."

"Bomp, bemp, bon, boom," I answered as I tried my best to hum out the tune from the movie.

---

[25] The movies are modern illustrations of the truths being presented. I am not endorsing everything in the movies referenced. If God can speak through a donkey (Numbers 22:28), he can speak through a movie as well.

Suddenly, the presence of God rapidly increased, encircling us and the porch.

Ruuush!

We felt like we were blasting off.

Gravity has a way of intensifying when God's glory shows up. We rocked back in our chairs so far that they hit the wall as an unseen force pushed against us. Even the ability to move becomes a workout under the weight of His glory.

The feeling reminded me of an old ride at the county fair called the "Gravatron." It would spin around so fast it would pin the riders against a padded wall. It felt like flying into orbit but came with an influx of dizziness afterward.

As the encounter intensified, tracking time became impossible. It felt like seconds but could have been a couple of minutes before we spoke.

Simultaneously, we turn our heads on our budge-less bodies towards one another.

"Do you feel that?"

"Yeah."

"What's going on?"

"It felt like we launched into heaven."

I had the feeling that I went somewhere quickly and then abruptly stopped.

We "sensed" that Jesus was very close.

Spiritual Sonar & Echolocation

Recently, I had a conversation with my friend, James. He was describing to me how he "sees" in the spirit. He said that he could feel what was there in the spirit and describe it to you but couldn't necessarily see it with his eyes.

I said, "like a spiritual sonar."

"Yes!" He answered with his eyes full of curiosity. "Just like that, a spiritual sonar."

Sonar uses sound pulses to measure depth and map out objects below the water's surface. Similarly, bats use echolocation to not only find their prey but identify their shape as they release soundwaves mid-flight.

In Jaxon and Avi's encounter with Jesus detailed in *Mystify*, they didn't see Him with their physical eyes, other than a flash of light, but they spiritually knew that the King's entourage was present. As He came near, they could see angels all around, on the tops of houses, fanning in all directions. This awareness led to unimaginable intensity when He walked in the door.

In our encounter, Scott and I echolocated Jesus with our spiritual sonar systems. In the same instance that we felt like the earth, house, and our bodies had moved through space and time. We perceived that Jesus came down from heaven and landed about 50 meters from us. Pinging off His presence, we noticed He was walking toward us. He was moving at an angle from left to right in our point of view. Yet, in no time at all, He was almost underneath the porch, near the big bush.

Behind the bush was a medium-sized tree, rising to eye-level with us on the porch. We had been out there for several hours as it was nearing 11:00 pm. And we heard not a sound from the bush or the tree. Nothing. There was no indication whatsoever that anything was around except for the occasional bugs and barking dogs.

Swooosh!

Suddenly—birds, hundreds of them—began flapping their wings, chirping, and flying into the air!

When Jesus showed up, creation responded with so much energy that it caught us off-guard. God's presence moved over the neighborhood like a fog rolling in or an upside-down mushroom cloud.

"Did the birds see Jesus too and get so excited that they flew into the air singing songs of praise?"

The number that flew out of the tree versus how many the tree could hold felt dramatically inconsistent. Was it a bird KOA campground for the night? It is hard to describe. None of it makes any logical sense. Thankfully, God isn't bound by logic. He does what He does, even if He created birds just to sing and fly into the night for us. Not all questions need to be answered. Imagination flourishes in the unknown. Yet, as we push off into the unexplainable, as Blake Healy says, "He adds clarity to mystery."

The whole event registered on the scale of scary—awesome—fear of the Lord type stuff!

"But wait, there's more."

As the birds swarmed into the air, invisible rings of light rippled across the spiritual sky as creation collided with Creator. Simultaneously, at the pond, just down the road, geese began honking wildly.

"What? Are there hundreds of geese too?'

We stared back and forth and up and down asking, both God and each other, "What is going on?"

"Honk, honk, honk!"

Louder and louder.

The chain reaction continued as echoes from creation spiraled outward, awakening further responses from sleepy creatures around the town.

The moment carried momentum that reverberated through the night sky. Holy awe and love created a fusion of nearness to our Lord. The encounter was beyond us, beyond reason, beyond time, and natural explanation.

Mesmerized, we exchanged exclamations of rapture while trying to decipher what was happening. Neither of us had an experience quite like this before.

At the point of ignition, when all the animals reacted to the presence of Jesus, it was as if Jesus Himself burst into a glory bomb and fanned out in all directions. Then, in the next moment, it was eerily still again. Somewhat normal gravity returned as we sat up and looked eyes in wonder.

"Did you feel Jesus?'

"Yeah, it was like He walked across the yard."

"I felt that too…Is He here still here?"

"I don't know?"

My spiritual sonar was still active, but He seemed to be everywhere.

I nervously stood and took careful steps over to the rail. I grabbed it and slowly leaned over and asked in a calm voice, "Jesus, are you in the bushes?"

It sounds funny, but I thought He might have been physically standing there. I did a double and triple take, leaning way over and then looking down through the spindles to make sure.

We were enamored by his glory when all of this was going on. We could feel heavenly currents and angelic activity. The reactions mirrored each other. Heaven splashed into earth, and earth splashed into heaven. Our senses picked up on the cause and effect of heaven and earth in unison. It was a four-dimensional experience. Scott had his encounter, as did I, along with our co-encounter in experiencing the whole phenomenon together as brothers. Jesus has His perspective too, which is above all. And there was the POV of the creatures themselves.

I mean, what were the birds thinking? Seriously!

"Fly, man, fly, the King is here! Sing, wing, fling yourself into the air. Do what He's created you to do!"

We tried our best to recap what just happened to each other, telling what we experienced like excited children who just left Disney World.

The sound of our wives coming home created another moment of holy unraveling as we were not sure if it was them, angels, or Jesus walking through the house.

We can pull many things out of this encounter that reveal the nature of heavenly encounters:

- Echolocation—spiritual sonar as a way to see and perceive in the spirit.
- Reverberation—progressive rings of influence. From just a couple of guys talking about Jesus on a porch, a chain reaction ignited as creation awakened to the awareness of their Creator.
- Transformation—the expanding of the rings is prophetic of city transformation. Awakened ones awaken others and spread the influence of kingdom family.
- Revival—As Jesus touches His family, those who were created to be in His family feel and respond to Him.

Activation

1. Imagine Jesus. Picture Him. What does He look like or sound like? Ask Him to show you.
2. Focus on Him. Ask Him to show you more. Ask to see His face, His hands, to hear His voice, feel his touch, and experience His heartbeat.
3. Your private experience with Him can become a revival that spreads across the city. Ask Him to show you your unique keys for city transformation.

CHAPTER 3 | REVERSING GRAVITY

He floated sideways in the air around three to five feet before he returned to earth…

The class, witnessing this event, erupted in praise, awe, and shock.

I was done teaching at that moment.

Having seen it with my eyes it would still take me another few years before I had the bravery to describe it as it was.

Levitation.

With such a word, one could immediately reject it, be intrigued by it, or demand an explanation. Questions are fair. They set us up for answers to be revealed. But the revelation comes not in the answer but in the journey through mystery that takes you there. For my part, I will give you the bigger story, including examples from the bible, church history, and even others from my life, but my aim will not be to convince you. I have only come as a messenger of the mysteries of God with hopes to invite you into discovering your own.

Limitless God, Limitless Power

Using words like "levitation" could solicit a "that's not in the bible" response. On the contrary, there are stories of reversing gravity, flying, walking on water, riding on the clouds, and much more. It depends on what we believe about God, ourselves, and the world. This worldview—*weltanschauung* will subconsciously become the belief system or lenses through which we experience reality. If God is a good, limitless Father, who invites us to join Him in the realm of impossibility, then something as minute as bending the laws of gravity, i.e., "levitation," will be seen as trivial on the grand scale of God's power.

A miracle occurs when the ordinary is infiltrated by the divine, creating something extraordinary. Miracles are often categorized as something only God could orchestrate. But this is the secret of Jesus:

Who, being in very nature, God...by taking the very nature of a servant...being made in human likeness...and being found in appearance as a man, He humbled Himself.

2 Philippians 2:6-9 TPT (excerpts)

Jesus, The Supreme, All Powerful, Most High God, Who reigns in the heavenly place, humbled Himself and took on the appearance of His own creation. He laid down His divinity. But He didn't hang it on a celestial coatrack. He placed it on us so that in Him taking on the earthly, we would be able to take on the heavenly.

Counterfeits and Broomsticks

Miracles are now both accessible and performable by the sons and daughters of God. Since Jesus paid to give us access to the supernatural, anything supernatural we experience will, by design, lead back to Him—The Great Designer. Anything supernatural that doesn't lead back to Him wasn't performed by Him. This is how we can distinguish what is God and what isn't: Does it lead to Jesus? And does it bear the fruit of His name?

As I stated earlier, Jesus says, "I am the Way, the Truth, and the Life. No one comes to the Father except through me" (John 14:6). If someone experiences something supernatural that leads not to Jesus, then there may have been a manifestation of the divine, but not the heavenly kind. It's real power, but it isn't accessed through Jesus. This approach is witchcraft—counterfeit spiritual authority. People who practice such things aren't operating in identity as God's sons and daughters who reign with Jesus in heavenly places (Eph 2:6). Therefore, they learn to manipulate the spiritual realm through rituals, spells, curses, energy, etc. The Ephesians themselves were bound in this until the Apostle Paul came to them, revealing the love and power of Jesus. Heaven showed up, and a city once bound in witchcraft became the city known for the most extraordinary miracles in the Book of Acts.[26]

The deceiver cannot create; he can only pervert. This is why the bible says the spirit of antichrist is in the world:

---

[26] Acts 19

By this you know the Spirit of God: every spirit that confesses that Jesus Christ has come in the flesh is from God, and every spirit that does not confess Jesus is not from God. This is the spirit of the antichrist, which you heard was coming and now is in the world already. Little children, you are from God and have overcome them, for he who is in you is greater than he who is in the world.

1 John 4:2-4 ESV

Anti means "another" or "against." This spirit is in operation when it is either pretending to be Jesus or directly opposing the ministry of Jesus. A spirit that pretends to be Jesus will never lead people to the Jesus of the bible, who performed signs and wonders, died, rose again, and ascended to restore His heavenly family. It will direct attention either to the person performing the miracle or direction away from the miracle. If someone isn't humble like we read about Jesus earlier, they may be influenced by this spirit. If they are performing the miraculous via spells, or something as outrageous as flying on a broomstick, then they aren't leading people to Jesus.

"Deception is very deceiving," as my spiritual father, Leif Hetland, often says. Sometimes, the fear that one can be deceived opens the door for deception. Knowing the enemy has counterfeit supernatural power causes many to fear any type of supernatural experience in hopes that they aren't deceived. In doing so, they begin to label anyone, even Christians who demonstrate biblically authentic miracles, as being deceived and/or demonic.

Accusations such as these do not originate in heaven. They do not mirror the ministry of Jesus.

When the bible says, "an angel of light will deceive many,"[27] it references "fallen sons of God"[28] who distort worship to Yahweh and brings it back to themselves. It had nothing to do with someone healing or performing miracles in Jesus name. It was calling out those who relied on the skill of speech rather than the power of God. All of Corinthians testifies to this. Paul rigorously defends the supernatural aspect of his ministry and goes on to say that only true apostles operate in signs and wonders.[29] It's quite simple: Healing in His name is Him. Accusation in His name is not. Someone may have bad character, but it won't stop Jesus from touching others throughout their life. But His goal is always for them to get healthy.

When hearing about "levitation," it doesn't always mean it's the enemy, antichrist, or witchcraft. Those are all counterfeits of the reality of a limitless God moving through a limitless people He calls His "glorious sons and daughters."[30] We need the wisdom of the Spirit so we can rightly identify what God is doing. So, don't be surprised

---

[27] 2 Corinthians 10:13

[28] Hebrew, *Elohim:* can refer to God (Elohim) of little "g" gods (elohim). These "sons of God" (Psalm 82) can refer to the "principalities and powers" (Eph 6); or the divine council that was designed to assist Yahweh in the governance of the nations, but instead chose to govern unjustly. Not all of them rebelled as some are still part of God's heavenly family. Reference: Michael S. Heiser, *Supernatural* (Bellingham: Lexham Press, 2015), p. 17-25.

[29] 2 Corinthians 12:12 – see page 121.

[30] Romans 8:19- In contrast to the divine "sons" of God mentioned above, "sons of god" in this verse refers to the family of God in the earth. Both the assignment of the divine family and the earthly family have to do with the governance of God's dominion or kingdom in both heaven and on earth. It was always God's intention that the heavenly and earthly families would rule and reign together. Heiser, *Supernatural,* p. 30-33. See also footnote 33.

when those who know Jesus, start doing the same things as Jesus, and even greater things!

> Believe that I live as one with my Father and that my Father lives as one with me—or at least, **believe because of the mighty miracles I have done.** I tell you this timeless truth: The person who follows me in faith, believing in me, will do the same mighty miracles that I do—**even greater miracles than these** because I go to be with my Father! For I will do whatever you ask me to do when you ask me in my name. And that is how the Son will show **what the Father is really like** and bring glory to him. Ask me anything in my name, and I will do it for you!

~John 14:11-13 TPT *emphasis mine*

Ecstatic Flight

Jesus, Himself is the Miracle Master. All things come from Him, flow through Him, and lead back to Him.[31] Dr. Robert Gladstone says that no matter where you place Jesus in the timeline, "He is the pinnacle of all creation."

> It is through him that we live and function and have our identity... "Our lineage comes from Him."

~Acts 17:28 TPT

There are several peculiar stories from His life that capture the eyes of imagination in ways that bend gravity:

---

[31] Romans 11:36

- Jesus walked on water and activated Peter to do the same (Mt 14, Mk 6, Jn 6). Did He levitate, transform matter, or walk on the hands of angels? Peter sees it, and in seeing it, he believes it. Belief combusts when added to faith, making his footsteps portals of heaven on earth. He followed the Master out onto the sea. In doing so, he reformed the earth in the pattern of the Son. Creation then responds the same way to Peter as it did to Jesus. The presence of the supernatural bent natural laws.

- Jesus ascends into heaven. We know that after His resurrection, He had His earthly body. During these 40 days of appearing to His disciples, He did several very astonishing miracles before finally ascending into heaven with His body (Acts 1), including walking through walls (Jn 20) and transforming His physical appearance (Lk 24). Miracles performed after His resurrection expand all possibilities. Once He returned from the dead, it removed caps from the disciples' minds, empowering them to experience Him in an expanded way. During His ascension, He was covered by a cloud. It would be easy to write this off as a "Jesus only" scenario, but to do that would be a means of cessationism. Everything He did was on purpose, revealing to creation the endless creativity and boundless (authentic) energy of His Father. In seeing Jesus ascend, they bore witness to a gravity-reversing moment, one Peter had already experienced and one in which other disciples and saints would also soon experience.

To suggest that Jesus could fly wouldn't be beyond the realm of possibility in the minds of most believers. To say that we could do it too is where you would usually get lost. But as we will see, many have. I have no interest in cataloging every levitation miracle in church history because others have already done it. But I will share a few of the ones that have captivated me.

A theme incorporated into *The Call for Revivalists* was how our culture looks to superheroes for examples of the supernatural. The idea that Superman can fly resonates in our culture. However, the idea that we can also bend the laws of gravity seems impossible. Is the concept of unassisted flight too much of a stretch, reserved only for comic book pages? No, we have One who is greater. Belief empowers us to think creatively. Creative thought is fueled through imagination. Imagination is unlocked by childlike wonder. Wonder enables us to push beyond the realm of logic and reason. If Jesus can fly and says we will do the same and *even greater things*, then Him empowering us in what He's already said should be believable.

Other Biblical characters have experienced levitation, or as the medieval saints called it, "ecstatic flight."

- Enoch walked with God, and he was no more. This refers to his earthly existence. How did he get to God? Did he fly or simply change dimensions? One moment he's here, and in the next moment, he steps into heaven? Books about his life reveal that he did indeed have out-of-this-world experiences.

- Elijah went to heaven via a whirlwind (2 Kings 2). A major theme I wrote about in *Mystify* was experiencing the wind of God. Elijah tapped into this on a whole other level. Were tornadoes his taxicabs? Before he ascended, it seemed to be common knowledge that he would be there one minute and gone the next, as the Spirit of the Lord would often carry him away (1 Kings 18). When I read things like this, I ask myself. "what did that look like? Did he fly, translocate, phase, etc.?" The story is in there for a reason, and my heart burns to search it out.

- There are numerous stories of flying saints. Two of my favorites are St. Joseph of Cupertino and St. Teresa of Avila. St. Joseph was known as "The Flying Friar." He would levitate for hours at a time and often float about the ground when traveling from one place to the next. Legend has it that he even flew up to help a group of saints place a cross atop the church's roof. St. Teresa would float up to several feet off the ground during her "Devotion of Ecstasy." Both were often hidden away because their raptures were so extreme.

For more on the mystical saints and other examples in church history of levitating and translocating, I recommend these resources:

- *Revivals and Revivalists* – David & Allessia Edwards
- *The New Mystics* – John Crowder
- *Beyond Human* – Justin Abraham

Even with these examples, such language still shocks our system because a lot of us grew up in a non-supernatural culture. And even though we love the stories of miracles we read in the bible, our Western worldview often compartmentalizes what we read from the reality of them occurring in our lives.

Mentone

While some may consider it wise to avoid writing a chapter about levitation, sometimes you got to "tell it like it is." It gives an honest assessment. Realizing this, I was able to recount similar occurrences in my history. Funny enough, if describing the events that occurred in the class were challenging to articulate, then this next story took two decades.

At 18, I was full of enormous passion for Jesus. Like a "deer panting for water," all I wanted was more of Him. I would often forego food, water, and sleep. It wasn't on purpose or to be spiritual. I was so hungry for Him that I forgot to eat. Yes, it is something I learned to steward over time, but it laid a solid foundation for the rest of my life to chase Jesus with "reckless abandon." This pursuit led me to a small mountain village of Mentone in Eastern Alabama, where our church held the summer youth camp.

"Mentone" was a buzzword amongst the youth group. It's where everyone got serious about God and underwent life change. My first trip there was the year before. I was "slain in the Spirit" for an hour and a half and saw visions of God. It sparked a fire that would carry me through my senior year of high school in 1998. After graduation, I returned as a youth leader in my first year of ministry.

During the twelve months in-between, my friend Brandon Weaver and I relentlessly prayed, sought God, went to the Brownsville Revival, and briefly lived together after his parents moved north. We were brothers united in spirit as God was all we could think about all day and night.

Coming into the extended weekend, we were so excited to get there, I may have drastically exceeded the speed limits on the back roads from metro Atlanta to rural Alabama.

The first night is usually an icebreaker before walls come down on the second night. It sets the atmosphere for spiritual transformation over the next two days. On the second night, there was an ease as expectations were that God would come and touch us.

The meeting flowed as usual with worship, the message, altar call, and a time of impartation. Brandon and I were on the prayer team and moved through the crowd of young people, laying hands on them. The presence of God quickly fell on all 300 of us. A glorious mess ensued as young men and women fell out all over the ground. All the feels and responses were present, from laughing to crying to demons fleeing and bodies shaking. Heaven was kissing earth and wrecking lives for the kingdom. Sometimes Brandon and I prayed for them together. Other times the crowd would separate us. The glory was so tremendous that we would barely get near people before they would shake and vibrate in His presence. I would go to extend my hand to touch them, and they would fly back with unusual force. As this began to happen more and more, I realized that what we were witnessing was moving beyond natural physics. Some seemed to be picked up into the air and moved backward. One foot, two feet, five feet! I was both exhilarated on the outside and in awe on the inside. What in the world was happening? It felt like we were in a glory bubble and that the natural realm was beginning to warp. Much more on that in a later chapter.

Amid the excitement, Brandon and I located each other again after a couple of hours had passed and the meeting was winding down. Or so it seemed. Nearly 100 were still on the floor, drenched in the power of God. We locked eyes as we joyously celebrated the moment and ran toward one another for a big ole brotherly hug.

I am not sure if we even touched each other.

It felt like we were each an oppositely charged magnet...

G-forces ensues...incoming floor

"Bang!"

"Crash," metal chairs crunch.

How did I get over the second row?

Dazed.

Confused.

"Where did Brandon go?"

Ah, he's lying over there, probably wondering where I went.

Now that I am writing about it, it must've looked like when two people in bubble suits run into each other. When we went to embrace, we were both picked up into the air and knocked back several feet, even flying completely over one row of chairs and into the next. One moment, we moved in one direction, and the next, we were moving in the opposite direction. I wouldn't have called it levitation back then. I didn't know what to say. I just told people that there was so much of God that we were picked up by the glory force and knocked backward.

Unusual, but not really. The Great Awakenings had many stories of people dramatically being moved by the Spirit. They didn't call it levitation or ecstatic flight like the saints, but they are very similar if you read the accounts. In fact, after experiencing this myself, I realized I had seen it before-people getting "extra" slain in the Spirit and flying back several feet. For sure, some of it seemed natural. But there were those occasions where you take a second look in your mind because what you just watched wasn't natural. It was supernatural.

Brandon and I picked ourselves up in acknowledgment of what just happened and began to rejoice at God shining upon us so spectacularly that night.

Electrify

From youth leader to revival pastor at Bethel Atlanta School of Supernatural Ministry (Bassm), fifteen years later, I found myself at another meeting where gravity would soon be reversed.

I've been careful to explain and build context up to now. Hopefully, your seatbelt is bucked because it's about to get swirly. My heart burns to not only teach about God moving supernaturally among His sons and daughters but to activate them to experience it too.

During the 2013 spring semester at Bassm, I was teaching revival history in the first-year class. I don't know how far into the teaching I made it. I get so fired up talking about Smith Wigglesworth, John G Lake, and Evan Roberts, that it's hard to keep myself and the class from jumping all in. And we were definitely not contained this night.

Suddenly, the awareness of God skyrocketed. The hair on my arms stood up as the fire of God covered my body. I began to see the students differently. I glared at them with pizazz. Holy Spirit was crackling on my body like Goku going Super Saiyan. Electricity filled the air as they recognized the shift in the atmosphere. The room was different than only seconds before.

Bassm met at Operation Mobilization at the time, and their main sanctuary was no stranger to the presence of God. No, it's not in a place: it's the people. But people filled with God will fill a place with His presence, and His presence will radiate in that place even if the people aren't present.

Several stories in *Mystify* would happen in this very room, from the wind blowing through the youth group to the building shaking. But the story I am telling here was the first one I was a part of in this storied space.

I surveyed both the students and my peers. There were over 80 people present. My session felt like we were on an accelerating escalator. When you're near the top, you prepare yourself to step off. If not, you bypass the moment. As a group, we were close. Some were more in tune than others, and that's okay. That's what family is for, to give us that nudge in the side when the time is right. Even now, as you read, you may be tracking as I've been preparing us to take a step. If not, here is your nudge!

Glancing back and forth, I felt a volcano erupting within me. I could not take it. I was pursuing a moment, but the moment arrived faster than I imagined. I wasn't nearly finished with my notes. Yet, my notes only existed for what was about to happen. Navigating the glory is as simple as yielding to the Spirit when He decides "it's time."

"God is here," I, well, I yelled at them. Not angrily, but it was most certainly full of vigor as it came from deep within. My mouth wasn't releasing breath onto vocal cords only; my whole body was animating the word of the Lord.

The teaching on revival was framed with the story of Elijah ascending into heaven and Elisha picking up the mantle to carry the move of God into the next generation.

"God is in this moment!" I voiced in a guttural ferocity.

"The mantle of revival is descending..."

"And like a touchdown pass from heaven, one of you is going to catch it!"

When I replay what happened next in my mind, it's like I can see it: Something flies from heaven to the earth. It didn't hit the young man in his seat, though. The God in the man and the God in the moment were on a collision course. However, he wouldn't wait for it to come. Like a wide receiver, he would rise to meet it.

There were three groups of chairs in the room—short, angled rows on the sides and a long, straight one in the middle. Travis Harris was sitting in the chair to my right at the end of the row closest to me. He always sat there. It wasn't more spiritual to be up front. He was burning and wanted to be close. During the night, he wasn't listening, rather, he was absorbing what both being taught was and what was happening in the room. If I was ready to step off, he was already jumping.

As soon as I said, "One of you is going to catch it," he began to vibrate rapidly in his chair like being plugged into an electrical current.

Crying out, his voice matched the shaking motion of his body, "whoooooo,oo,oo,oo,oo,oo,aa" as the sound curved between pitches.

When the electrification hit him, his body went straight as he shook, causing him to lean back in his chair. Only, instead of sliding down, he went up, levitating about three feet into the air.

Next, he floated to his left around four or five feet as the vibrations continued before landing on the ground and pulsating in the fetal position.

"He caught it!" I exclaimed loudly.

The reaction from the student body was like turning up the volume on an amplifier. Some jumped from their seats and lifted their hands to heaven as others fell to the ground with their faces on the carpet. Gentle adoration married exhales of praise. Several cried out "Jesus," as others released moans from the Holy Spirit. It was both loud and quiet after a few moments. Some let out verbal expressions here and there, while most sat in silence at the awesomeness of God.

How do you respond after seeing something like this? It was a substantial wonder that 95% of the people in the room witnessed. It was as if a holy stupor or gaze captured us.

A pause.

"Don't miss this moment!" I instructed.

"Travis rose up to heaven to intercept the pass, and heaven's not done."

I felt to help them navigate the presence in the room as Travis was still pulsating with electric life on the floor. My inner dialogue with the Lord reminded me of how Dr. Gladstone used to encourage us to allow the Spirit to "animate our bodies" before the Lord.

"Allow the Spirit to move through you, to animate your body to express what He's doing in the room."

"It could be singing and dancing or sitting quietly, but whatever it is that He's asking you to do, Do It! Heaven's next move could be to flow through you."

I paced back and forth in front of them as the room seemed to bend back and forth. We were in a kingdom culture, but we found ourselves in-between worlds. Heaven and Earth were dancing together as a vessel for God's sons and daughters to experience Him in ways that were beyond articulation. I always expect God to move, and I was charged to speak on revival that night. So much so that I had spent extra time with the Lord that week in eager anticipation. But. I didn't know I would watch someone float up out of their chair at school that night.

"One of you has a song in you. I can feel it."

"Release it!"

"Just as Travis caught hold of it, your song is key to where we go next. It's okay; we are family here. Let it out."

A student in the middle rose to their feet. I don't remember who it was, only that they were brave and allowed heaven's song to flow from their innermost being and out of their lips.

ANIMATION.

Like lighting a pack of Black Cat Firecrackers, many students stood and began to sing along. Some sang along with the first student's song. Others began to release their own sounds as a spontaneous choir emerged. All got into it. Risking it inspires others to express themselves. Freedom baptized their hearts and catapulted them into new places in God. So, it went on for a long time as I occasionally coached them into synchronicity with what I felt the Lord was doing. The more they released, the louder and more expressive they became. I couldn't believe it; this was really happening. It felt like one of the Holy Spirit breakouts from Brownsville. They were standing, shouting, walking, running, jumping, and moving all over the room. There were people at the altar and people laid out in the back.

Then, a rush filled the room as His weighty glory entered. The unison from before scattered into a "no-holds-barred" frenzy as they grew more and more intense in their pursuit of God. At this point, I was sitting on the small stage with my feet on the floor. The mic rested in my right hand on my knee. I looked over to see Jenn Stockman, First-Year Director, army crawling towards me. So, I stuck out the microphone as I thought, "I'll let her grab it if she makes it here." She was the authority in the room, so I assumed she wanted to share something. After a minute, I realized that she didn't make it. She got sloshed in the glory along the way.

Next, things got hazy. I abandoned all attempts to help them get the most out of what God was doing because God Himself had gotten hold of all of them. I looked at the back wall and saw a spinning cloudy-like portal opening. I vibrated as it appeared to be bending in and out of itself. I thought about jumping in. My friend Jeremy saw me trance out and later asked what in the world I was looking at, but I couldn't describe it. God was doing stuff all over the room. We gave way to Him to have His way. Over an hour and a half went by as we could feel the reality of the moment reach a transition point as breaktime had come upon us.

Students to this day still tell of this breakout as Travis's experience has become quite legendary. "He flew out of his chair and into the wall!" is how some describe it, but from where they were sitting, it probably appeared that way.

I later asked Jenn what she was doing when she was army crawling; "Did you want the mic? I had it ready to give to you."

"I don't know," she answered. "It just felt like a good idea at the time…I just wanted to be closer to the glory."

Again

Teaching at School of Revivalists in 2021, I told this story to the first-year students. They were a hungry group, believing for revival. As I shared, the same feeling of fire that came upon me eight years before, hit me. I thought, "Are you about to wreck us again, God?" Students started to feel it as they filled the room with animated expressions.

Out of the corner of my eye, a group reacted to something. They sat to my right in a similar position as Travis. Gasps and giggles filled the air as an empty seat in the middle of them moved. I thought one of them was leaning on it or something. What I didn't see was it float into the air. I only saw it move right at the point that it came down. They told me that one student had his arm on the back of the chair, and it started to rise into the air as I was talking about Travis. Most of the room saw it as another chain reaction went off. Again, I was done teaching as the presence of God filled the room with all the same reactions. Weeping, wailing, laughing, and crying as an array of emotions flooded in.

My wife, Allessia, was so overcome by the weighty glory that she began to army crawl (just like Jenn) towards the restroom as she could not stand. One student, who had never experienced the glory of God like this before, grabbed her and held on tight. Waves of tears flowed down her face as she experienced the baptism of love for the first time.

God did it again, not the exact same, but He came to stamp His authenticity on such an extreme story, declaring, "This is me," through releasing another wonder.

If you're wondering why—Because He is God.

Why would a person levitate or chair float in response to the story? Because He is God and can do anything.

What is the fruit?

Lives were transformed, all giving glory to God and falling exceptionally more in love with Jesus. He shows us that He can do amazing things. All of the stories in this chapter and this book aren't about the stories themselves. They are all about Jesus. They stretch me even though I was there. They call me higher when I lose sight of His wonder and majesty. They are memory stones that prophesy to me God's desire to do extraordinary things in and through my life. He desires to do the same for you. When you look to Him, you will see and experience wonderfully supernatural manifestations happening all around you.

Activation

Prayerfully read through St. Teresa's four stages of prayer and ask the Lord to activate each experience.

1. Mental Prayer – Concentration and contemplation, removing the soul from outwardness.

   - This is the place where you focus on the Lord, removing all distraction and pushing out all thoughts apart from Him.

2. Prayer of Quiet – Human will is lost as one moves in to a supernatural state.

   - You are now with Him, and He is with you, a mutual enjoyment.

3. Devotion of Union – ecstatic state, absorption into God, a sweet slumber in which only memory and imagination are left functioning.

   - This is the state where most of us stop. For me, I would describe it like being slain in the Spirit or caught up in a trance.

4. Devotion of Ecstasy or Rapture – a passive state in which the feeling of the body disappears. Sometimes such an ecstatic flight that the body is lifted into space, caught up into pleasure with God where all awareness of this world is gone. Frequently, she would reach this trance-like state in mass, levitating for up to half an hour at a time.

   - Here, you go beyond the realm of God and enter into God Himself. It's where all natural limitations end, and the limitless reality of God permeates your entire being. He is all there is.[32]

---

[32] David & Allessia Edwards, *Revivals & Revivalists* (Revivalism: Atlanta, 2018), p. 24-25.

CHAPTER 4 | GALAXY QUEST

In the next moment, I found myself spinning around a galaxy faster than the speed of light...

No. I am not an astronaut. Although, flying through space is something that would be exhilarating. Maybe we will even see it happen in our generation as both Richard Branson and Jeff Bezos recently took civilian craft beyond our atmosphere. I've always been a big fan of Sci-fi, from Star Trek and Star Wars to lesser-known outer space adventures. I begin a chapter from *The Call for Revivalists* by stating that I want to explore the depths of God the same way Captain Kirk explored space. I've always been fascinated by looking up. The sky and stars fill me with wonder.

In the same way, the ancient world looked skyward, which represented both the realm above and the realm of God. The Apostle Paul references this when he mentions going to the third heaven—he went beyond the starry (lit. *astral* i.e., "cosmic") plane to the one above. So, I believe our Creator put a desire in us, His Creation, a desire to experience Him both in heaven and on earth.

I love the Bible Project channel on YouTube. They illustrate biblical stories in a way easily understood by children while releasing eye-opening revelation to grown-ups. In addition, I love their series on Spiritual Beings.[33] As I watched it, I realized that the way I viewed the spiritual world and the things I was taught, even as a Charismatic Christian were, only fragments of how the ones who wrote the bible viewed it.

Putty Putman PhD, author of *Kingdom Impact* and founder of School of Kingdom Ministry, has a fantastic grasp on how the understanding of the ancient supernatural worldview and how it impacts the Gospel of the Kingdom today. After interviewing him for my YouTube series, "3 Questions," about these things, I asked him if he had seen The Bible Project. Wide-eyed, he said he loved it and then recommended that I check out Dr. Michael Heiser, author of *Unseen Realm* and *Supernatural.* Dr. Heiser's books and teachings unlock this paradigm on a whole new level.[34] He reveals the spirituality of the ancient world. The bible is interconnected with other ancient cultures, which doesn't invalidate it; rather, it makes it more authentic.

I am in no way going to try to replicate his teachings, but I encourage you to check them out and make your own decisions about how they might apply to your life. They both challenged me and upgraded my view of what the bible says about the spiritual realm. Ironically, this

---

33 Spiritual Beings Series: https://youtu.be/cBxOZqtGTXE (scan qr code)
34 See footnotes 28 and 30.

only proved some of the supernatural experiences I had, including the opening teaser of this chapter, which, as I always do, will finish at the end of the chapter. Unfortunately, when sharing about the heavenly realm and the wonders of God present there, it's hard to use earthly language to describe it. The problem of communicating extravagance is why the biblical authors used metaphor in writing about apocalyptic experiences.

Apocalyptic Encounters

Divergent to popular culture, *apocalypse* doesn't mean the "end of the world" but an "unveiling." It became eschatological because of modern misreading of the Book of Revelation from a Western worldview. Revelation does reference the end of the age, but that is not its only timeframe. Sadly, this is the one-dimensional way most view it. *Apocalypse* is so much more. It's seeing from God's perspective, including the past, present, and future.

Again, Apocalyptic Literature in the bible refers to an encounter when someone leaves the earthly space and experiences the heavenly space. The Bible Project illustrates by envisioning the Hebraic worldview with two circles: one above and one below. The one above is the heavenly space; the one below is the earthly space (FIG 1). These two circles intersected at a place called "Eden." Eden is the realm of God's pleasure where heaven touches earth. It's also the place where God's heavenly family and earthly family would connect and spread the rule of the family over the earth and throughout the cosmos.

At the fall, humankind lost their place in this realm (although, some still accessed it through faith). Jesus came to restore God's sons and daughters to their heavenly space. Now, His family can continue commission from the Garden to fill all creation with the knowledge of the glory of God.[35]

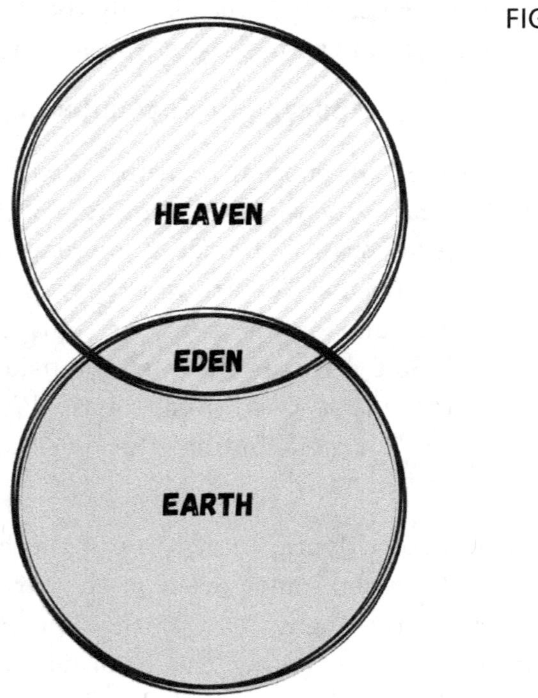

The blueprint in Genesis shows us our destiny as God's glorious sons and daughters. The realms or spaces: 1st heaven, 2nd heaven, and 3rd heaven are to be inhabited and ruled by God's cosmic family (FIG 2). Both on earth and in the 2nd heaven, the forces of darkness[36] still try to destroy God's plan, but he has raised up His

---

[35] Hebrews 11, Genesis 1-2, Ephesians 2:6, Matthew 28, Habakkuk 2:14
[36] Ephesians 6

Ekklesia (church) to drive out their chaos through His divine order (cosmos), revealing heavenly family.[37] The church is part of the Kingdom of God. Eden's design was to fill the cosmos with the Creator's rule, and, as the ekklesia, we complete this assignment through the preaching of the Gospel and the demonstration of the kingdom. The End Game is for all creation to be filled with the glory of God.

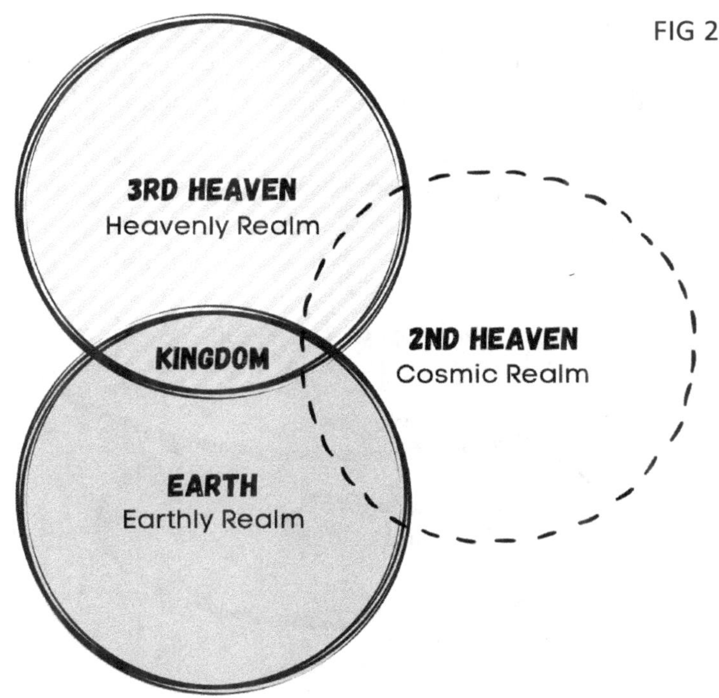

When someone in the Old Testament would have an experience in the 3rd heaven, it was classified as "apocalyptic." Enoch, Ezekiel, Isaiah, Daniel, and others had these experiences.[38] In the New Testament, you see

---

[37] Matthew 16, John 3, Ephesians 5:32; 3:10
[38] Genesis 5, Ezekiel 1, Isaiah 6, Daniel 7, various psalms and minor prophets.

it on the Mount of Transfiguration, in Revelation, and when Paul mentions his experience, although his only description of it was that it was indescribable.[39] My adjective count for this book is already exhausted because words fail to capture the beauty of its majesty when seeing heaven.

Now that I've laid the foundation for understanding these realms, we can talk about what it's like to explore them. You can't blast off in one of Elon Musk's SpaceX rockets and fly into God. God doesn't live somewhere in the universe; the universe lives somewhere in God. However, you can ascend[40] (FIG 3).

FIG 3

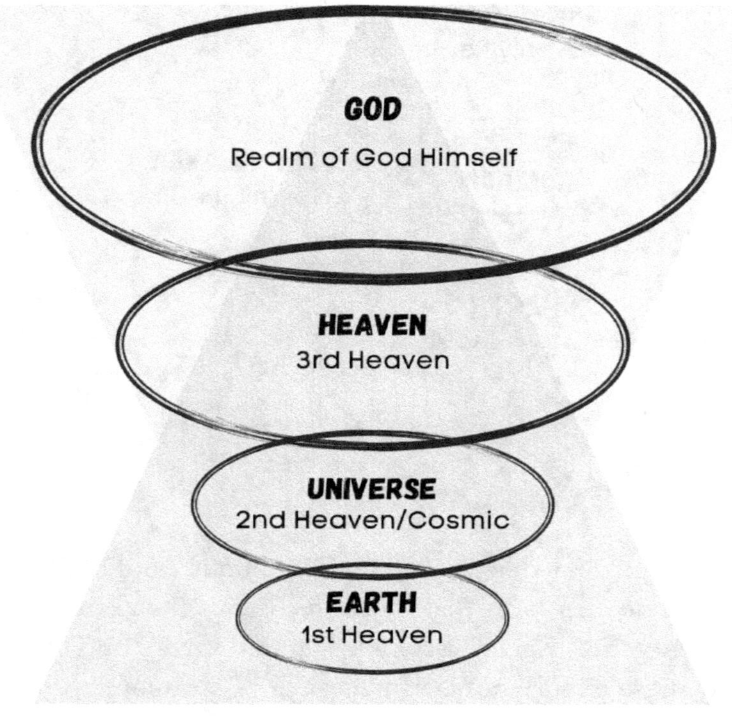

[39] Matthew 17, Revelation 4:1, 2 Corinthians 12
[40] Psalm 24, 2 Kings 2, Acts 1

We see examples of people in scripture and church history interacting in these realms. The Realm of Eden is always depicted as a mountain. This is the metaphorical or mystical "Mountain of the Lord." The darker shade triangle in FIG 3 symbolizes those who ascend, whereas the funnel shows the flow of heaven to earth. Together, they show the Rule of the Kingdom covering all creation. Psalm 24 is an invitation to ascend, to experience God in His realm. And, as David reveals, those who do will transform their generation like Jacob, who dreamed of Heaven touching earth.

> The earth is the Lord's, and everything in it,
>   the world, and all who live in it;
> for he founded it on the seas
>   and established it on the waters.
>
> Who may ascend the mountain of the Lord?
>   Who may stand in his holy place?
> The one who has clean hands and a pure heart,
>   who does not trust in an idol
>   or swear by a false god.
>
> They will receive blessing from the Lord
>   and vindication from God their Savior.
> Such is the generation of those who seek him,
>   who seek your face, God of Jacob.

Psalm 24:1-6 TPT

Jesus is the ultimate example. He is the embodiment of Psalm 24, The Son of David. The Realm of God Himself was inside of Jesus when He walked the earth. In fact, He is the ladder that Jacob saw, connecting the earth to heaven.[41] To see Him was to see into and experience that realm. All realms are in Him, and in Him, we have access to all realms.

> The true God is the Creator of all things. He is the owner and Lord of the heavenly realm and the earthly realm, and he doesn't live in man-made temples. It is through him that we live and function and have our identity.
>
> Acts 17:24; 28a TPT

Other translations say, "In Him we live and move and have our being." In Christ, we have access to all mystery, depth, and knowledge, for the Holy Spirit reveals these to us.[42]

We also see what it looks like when these realms collide, as I've already shared a couple of stories. You don't need a spacesuit; you need a faith suit. If you believe the bible is trustworthy, then the stories it contains are both real and invite you to explore the mysteries waiting to be unveiled. The bible says in the Gospel of John that Jesus was both in heaven and on earth. Likewise, we are seated next to Him in heavenly places while also on the earth.

I heard stories about those in our lifetime who've experienced the apocalyptic. Travis Harris, St. Teresa of Avila, and St. Joseph of Cupertino were examples of the weightlessness that manifests when these realms intersect. All of the ones I've written about had one aim— Jesus. The cross itself is an intersection. In experiencing

------

41 Genesis 28:12, John 1:51
42 1 Corinthians 2:10

Jesus, they began to experience everything in Jesus and all that Jesus died to make available to us. *Mesmerize* is simply a ramp to help release that which has already been released through Jesus. I believe Teresa's fourth stage of prayer is an attempt to illustrate and activate apocalyptic experiences. She went there and wanted to leave a trail for others to follow.

Another is Ian Clayton, a modern-day mystic who has translocated to places on earth, the cosmos, and the heavenly realms. After listening to podcasts and seeing him in person a couple of times, it created a connection point for me to ignite my galactic quest. Hearing him talk about experiencing the realm of the stars awakened my inner child who got excited to watch "Star Trek: The Next Generation" with my dad when growing up. But I wasn't content just hearing about it. I wanted to go and see.

"Is it possible?" the adult mind calculates.

"What if it is possible!" Childlike faith answers.

Again, we have 21st Century lenses that cause us to view everything, even faith, through logic and reason. Kids don't let information stop them from pursuing. They aren't satisfied with information only; they want to do it. Likewise, I may hear about how exhilarating a rollercoaster is, how it works, and how long the ride lasts, but I merely have facts without experience unless I try it.

In the worldview of the biblical writers, these experiences were possible. Not only that, but they were also common. And, if we read the bible as they intended, we will find that experiences of people going to the heavenly realms happened a lot more than we both realize, and most modern translations suggest.

"Rapture," "trance," and "ecstasy" are all rooted in the same Greek word, *ekstasis.* It has several layers of meaning, such as "being carried away in the mind"- a trance-like state, "being carried away in the body"- translocation, or "to stand outside oneself"- being carried away in the spirit. Often in the New Testament, *ekstasis* is translated as "astonishment" or "amazement." In seeing it used this way, we realize that these moments had way more impact than believers simply "getting excited." They had trance-like encounters. These encounters included experiences in all three realms (first, second, third heaven).

I shared the story of my trip to the cosmos on Supernatural Stories, an ISN production where guests talk about their heavenly testimonies. While most were blessed and encouraged, some got triggered by how I described my encounter.

"That's astral projection!"

"That's the devil…we need more 'discernment' in the body."

I appreciate their desire to use discernment but getting triggered by one thing doesn't mean it is counterfeit, as I stated in the last chapter and in the preface. Yes, some have supernatural experiences in the second heaven, which is referred to as the "astral" realm in their description. Astral is just a word used to describe outer space or the soul (nonphysical) realm. Many use the term "astral projection" to describe out-of-body experiences. However, we wouldn't ascribe astral projection to Paul's trip to heaven, where he had no idea if he was in or out of his body. Of course not. We know that he is a believer, so he must have experienced rapture. He talked about and gave glory to God afterward, certifying the authenticity of the encounter. Definitionally speaking, it's the same type of experience, but the false is sourced from the second heaven, while the genuine originates in the third heaven.

The difference is that those in New Age, the occult, and witchcraft commonly practice astral projection. They have real supernatural experiences, but they don't go through Jesus to access the heavenly realms. They use demonic spirits. The devil is real and uses real supernatural power to trick people. His goal is to pervert biblically-based supernatural encounters in an attempt to both invalidate and make people afraid of them. In other words, the enemy wants to falsify the real by creating a counterfeit and then claiming that the genuine encounter is also counterfeit. His forces of darkness reign in these heavenly spaces (Eph 6). But we are the imagers of God. We reign from heaven to earth, seated at the right hand of Jesus, with the devil and his domain under our feet (Eph 2). We have real access to these realms in Jesus. And, not just that, we rule and reign there with Him as sons and daughters of the High King. Remember, this isn't just a hypothetical picture. We are not earthbound. As this scripture states, we are heavenly beings, transforming the world into His image.

Did you know that the word for "world" in the famous verse, John 3:16, is cosmos? "For God so loved the 'cosmos' that He gave His Son..." "Cosmos" is the "divinely intended order" of all creation. Jesus didn't come to rescue people and destroy a planet, He came to redeem His Father's design over all creation- earth, the universe, and the cosmos. Cosmos was also used by Pythagoras to describe the stars—universe, outer space, etc. He felt there was an order to it. The *Kosmos*—all creation, including the universe—was so loved by God that Jesus redeemed it. The cosmos is reset in His image as we rule and reign in these heavenly places.

The great evangelist Billy Graham once said[43] when talking to famous talk show host Johnny Carson about visualizing heaven, that he believes that we won't just be "sitting under palm trees with beautiful girls fanning us, as some people envision heaven. I believe we will be going from planet to planet and from one part of the universe to the other. I think we will be able to go as fast as thought. I think that we are going to have other worlds to conquer. We are going to have tremendous enterprises to do on other planets. And I think there are many indications in the bible about this." I agree.

Billy Graham painted a picture of eternity for an audience who wondered what it would be like after death. However, I believe that it's very clear from the Hebraic worldview within the bible and from those who've done it that we have access now. We don't have to wait for death to access something that Jesus already died to give us. The universe seems endless from our human perception. Why did God create it? It goes back to His plan or cosmos in Genesis. To subdue creation and multiply. We were

---

[43] Tonight Show, Billy Graham sits down with Johnny Carson, 1973: https://youtu.be/RdkbNGCp1G4 (scan qr code) 

created to expand the reign of His kingdom both naturally and spiritually across the cosmos.

Reality Revealed

Continuing our consideration of Ephesians, the believers there were a very peculiar bunch. Ephesus was the capital of paganism and witchcraft in the first century until a short-unibrow Hebrew named Paul limped into town and dethroned their gods. Upon hearing his message, they burned millions of dollars worth of witchcraft and demonic books and became known for a heavenly book. They went from having counterfeit supernatural authority to having genuine supernatural authority.[44] Their eyes opened to the truth of the spiritual realm. The Light exposed that the level of supernatural power they experienced was nothing compared to Jesus.

Just because they were previously operating in darkness, it didn't mean that their newfound supernatural power in the Holy Spirit was also counterfeit. Just because there are people who operate in darkness today doesn't invalidate genuine supernatural experiences in the Holy Spirit.

That same, small in earthly stature yet large in spirit, Jew—the Apostle Paul—even went as far as to say that the purpose of the church (ekklesia) was to make known the mystery (heavenly family) of God to the rulers and authorities in heavenly places.[45] We are not being the true governing family the Father intended unless we are ruling and reigning with Christ in heavenly places.

---

[44] Acts 19

[45] Ephesians 3:10- We now reign above the *elohim* who disobeyed their heavenly assignment. We are God's imagers in heavenly places, removing their chaos with cosmos.

Ephesians is all about who the church is and what she is called to do—her identity and authority. These aren't earthbound, un-experiential principles. They are the revelation of who we really are. We are called to reign in the heavenly realms, to have apocalyptic encounters, dethrone demonic entities, and shine the light of Christ across the cosmos.

I've covered the stories Paul's trip to heaven, the redemption of Ephesus, Elijah's ascent, and others to make known to us a supernatural reality and way of life. Hearing this for the first time may be shocking, but do we believe the bible or not? It's just as easy to read the bible and not really believe it as it is to fall in love with a story in one of our favorite movies. We know the movie is a set but love the story. Likewise, we love the story of the bible but don't think it can happen in real life.

Several movies address this paradox, such as The Matrix and Inception. But, as epic as they are, sometimes it takes a comedy to add a real-life connection. Actor, Tim Allen, plays actor Jason Nesmith, who plays Captain Peter Quincy in the movie "Galaxy Quest," a spoof on Star Trek. He, being an actor, played someone who went to space like Captain James T. Kirk, but it was only a show, just like Trek.

One day, a group of aliens, believing his TV show adventures were real, show up at his door asking him to save their people. He thought it was just another gig but soon found himself on a spaceship. He went from playing a space hero on TV to finding himself in outer space. He went from "earthbound thinking," as Graham Cooke often describes, to cosmic thinking. The movie illustrates the drastic shift in reality the Ephesians experienced when Paul showed up like an alien and transported them into a higher realm.

In reading this, you may find yourself in the same position. As I pursued the Lord and found that some have tasted and seen God in the cosmos, I knew I had to be next in line for "beam me up Scotty."

I want to experience all of Jesus, including the place He made for me in the heavens. I want to follow in the footsteps of Paul, Enoch, Daniel, Ezekiel, and John. I hear stories from Ian and people like Justin Abraham, and I know there is more. With the bible as a guide and these testimonies as inspiration, I used these ingredients to tune my prayer life for a season and found myself in a season of awe as I pressed into the unknown.

Our imagination is a God-given powerful tool that ignites our spirit within us. Author, Judy Franklin, calls it the "eyes of our spirit." When I read the bible, I imagine what it was like to be there and put myself into the story. I do the same with testimonies. This creates expectation, faith, and belief, synchronizing my body, mind, and spirit in a position for more. If I can see His world in my spirit, I can frame His reality around me in the natural.

Prayer of Ascension

The Lord's Prayer contains all the necessary components to ignite a supernatural lifestyle and release heaven on earth, "Your kingdom come, your will be done, on earth as it is in heaven," (Mt 6:9-10). When we ascend into His kingdom, we align in His will (cosmos). Then we reign from heaven to earth, expanding His rule as His ekklesia. In praying this prayer, we transition from the circle of the earth to the circle of heaven. It is an act of unification between the two. We are earthly beings in heavenly spaces who reign as heavenly beings in earthly spaces.

FIG 4

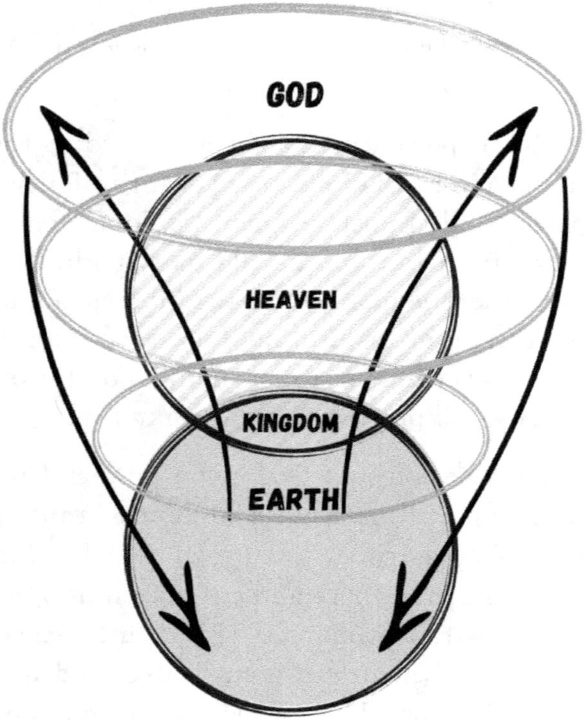

We can also vie metanoia this way. When we change from earth to heaven through to heaven to earth, the impossibilities of the earthbound mindsets fade as the possibilities of heaven-renewed mindsets invade. It creates a cycle—when our minds transform, we ascend. As we ascend, the earth is transformed through the revealing of God's sons and daughters reigning as mothers and fathers on the earth. See FIG 4 (Visualizing the Lord's Prayer).

The image of Christ is also illustrated by a circle (FIG 5). If it originates in Him (His Image), it must conclude in Him (cosmos). Anything that doesn't complete or "hit the mark" in Him is sin—outside the intended image. When we see who we are as originating in Him, we will find His will in us and live in His image as His imagers. It all comes together and completes the circle of His image in heaven and on earth.

FIG 5

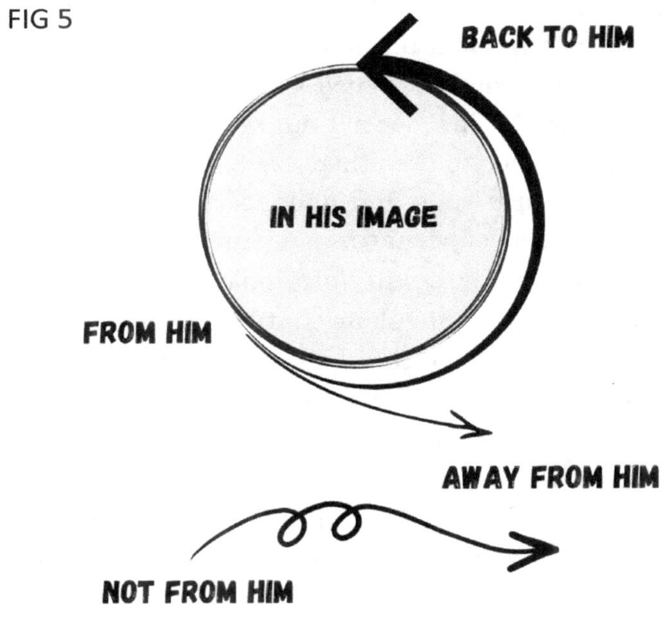

Knowing my place as a son activates a supernatural belief system. I can see as He sees, transforming earthbound perspectives into a limitless heavenly worldview. If I visualize my place in the Lord's prayer— in the heavenly realm—it will activate His reality in my earthly space or trance-port me to his realm.

There was a group of ancient Jewish mystics called Merkabah Mystics.[46] They would pray and meditate about Ezekiel's encounter in the belief that they too would experience God on His mobile throne (Merkabah or chariot). They wanted to activate the encounter. How do we apply this today? All encounters go through Jesus. He is the door the genuine experiences in the heavenly realms.

Over the centuries, the world and even the occult have used even stolen terms that originated in genuine supernatural encounters, such as "mystic," "Merkabah," and "meditate." This doesn't make them all "evil" or deceptive. It's time to take them back and reveal who the true supernatural sons and daughters are. The church has always been supernatural. I am not talking about taking New Age or occult terminology and making it Christian. My aim is to show that the origin of many of these things began in either Israel or the church and has been lost, confiscated, or misunderstood over time. Many have become afraid of them and classify them all as demonic, even when it is a solid biblically-based experience found throughout church history. Many claim these experiences are New Age when the New Age has only been around since the 1970s. People were shaking and vibrating in God's presence in the Jesus Movement, The Great Awakenings, Medieval monasteries, and the

---

[46] Merkabah Mysticism originated between 800 and 500 BC. It centered around the experience in Ezekiel, chapter one, where he encountered the mobile throne. Over the years, its Jewish development focused on apocalyptic literature and theology, such as the idea of seven levels of heaven. This belief was prominent in Pauls' day as part of Hellenistic thought, which is why he specifically points out there are three levels of heaven. Many have taken this concept far away from its original intent and even from God Himself in the thousands of years since. This, however, doesn't invalidate it, but extreme caution and guidance are needed in its understanding, application, and study.

early church. God is awesome, and when He moves on His people, they feel His power in a very real, very tangible way. Don't miss out on what God is doing today because a small bubble of people don't (or refuse to) understand it. The pattern is clear in the bible and church history. True encounters always come from Him and lead back to Him, revealing His image in the earth.

"Activation" is another term that gets a bad rap. I once had someone say I was "evil" and "not from God" because of the title of my book, *Activating a Prophetic Lifestyle*. They didn't even read it, just triggered by the title and the use of "activate." I have listed both biblical and historical contexts for activations. They are not a new invention of the Charismatic movement; they are part of the Jewish antiquity. The distance between the natural and supernatural wasn't blocked by theoretical science. Being mystic and activating supernatural encounters isn't a bunch of deceived people operating in "kundalini energy." It's both the ancient and modern way God relates to His people. The Kundalin[47] myth is no different than the Pharisees identifying the manifestation of the Holy Spirit in Jesus's life as "Beelzebub" (Mt 12). Experiencing the spiritual world was foundational to the understanding the writers had in mind for both testaments of the bible. It's the intent of the Lord.

The Lord's prayer is an activation. Yet, the church has spent millennia reciting something Jesus told them not to (Mt 6) while missing out on the experiences hidden

---

[47] See "Supernatural Christianity" (Kundalini in the Church Debunked) for further explanation, https://youtu.be/eUh2LW-opZo (scan qr code) 

within. Saints, it's time to go for it and return to our history and launch into our destiny as supernatural sons and daughters. Jesus' prayer is key to apocalyptic realities. Praying from the reality of the Lord's prayer opens up His world to ours. It may at first be only imagination, but it will spiral upwards into a vision, a trance, and an out-of-body or otherworldly experience.

Up, Up, and Away

Sitting in a comfy chair one night at our Pastors, Greg and Nancy Tankersley's house, I turned my gaze to the cosmos during a prayer meeting. I began to imagine the cosmos. It was blurry and far-off at first, but then, in a split second, it seemed to rush at me at warp speed.

One minute, I was sitting in the chair in the little house in Acworth, GA, and in the next, I was spinning around a galaxy faster than the speed of light. I realized it was no longer an imagination or activation. I guess I found my ascent as St. Teresa instructed. And just like Dorothy in the Wizard of OZ, I "wasn't in Kansas" anymore…I was somewhere in the stars.

"Up, up, and away," is an old saying that describes Superman's leap into flight. Ecstatic flight has its own feeling of "up, up, and away." Todd Shockley is a friend who leads worship and can take those in his sessions into the glory realms. I remember hearing him use this line as a prophetic declaration in Atlanta in early 2019 at a Brian Guerin meeting as he navigated people through the streams of glory. It made so much sense to me to view it that way. The constant theme of this book is about going into the heavens and experiencing God. I share these stories to make the lessons of St. Teresa attainable.

The experience of God is not distant. Misty Edwards says, "He is as new as turned attention." You can be in a chair in Georgia in one minute, and in the next, somewhere in the cosmos, lost in Him, in the next. Up, up and away!

The impact of the encounter hit me like a wave in the ocean that knocked me off my feet. My senses were askew as stars like water rushed all around me.

Flash.

Light.

Movement.

"Wahhha!"

Fighting to orientate, I said to myself, "I can't handle this."

"Errrrrr," like the sound of brakes locking in a car and bang, I was back in the chair.

It was less than five seconds.

I am slowing the story way down to give a place of connection. I could easily say it the way I experienced it, but I want to give you space to breathe.

As with scenarios like this, there's always more than meets the eye in the initial. I felt like I was in a bottle of bubbly, swooshing around. I could tell there was a galaxy, which was my focal point. Usually, points like this are the ground or the sky. They keep you stable in your environment. My body was free of gravity, so I focused on the ball of light at the core of this away place in the universe.

No sooner had I hit the chair (which I never really left) than I thought, "No, I want to see more!"

Ruuussshhhh!

Instantly, I was back, spinning around the same galaxy. It felt like I was going the speed of light, but I am sure that the speed of light was much faster than my orbit. As Billy Graham described it, I did arrive as fast as the speed of thought. This is also how they traveled across the cosmos in *A Wrinkle in Time* as they would "tesser" to create 4th-dimensional wormholes with their minds. Author, Madeleine L'Engle, was a Christian who tried to show all that was accessible in Jesus, but many misunderstood it as a devaluation of Him. Rather, it illustrated that the others were special because of Him. And in Him, we have an open door to the heavenlies.

It was all golden. The stars shone bright white as the galactic center looked like a giant celestial pearl emanating varying hues. Seeing Jesus in my Sky Dream encounter, which I'll refer to more later, was similar to viewing a galaxy with all of His splendor. I can see how the cosmos proclaim His eminence, and the invitation to explore them is likewise an invitation to explore Him. Three to five times around could have just as easily have been ten to fifteen times around as natural observance was tasking in this suspended environment. I felt like I was hanging on to the back of a roller-coaster with feet kicking about in the air.

"It's tooooo muucc..."

Sentence unfinished.

Back in the chair.

"Nooo, I want to see mooorrreeee."

Whoosh.

Spinning, stars, lights.

Back and forth I went, maybe seven, maybe eleven times. Every time was a rush. Every time it was too intense. Every time I came back almost as soon as I arrived. Hitting the chair caused the same reaction, an urge to go back. I was a cosmic yo-yo.

The whole encounter felt extremely quick, but I knew at least fifteen minutes went by in the natural. In my last trip or two, I remained in the moment longer than all the previous ones, which is where I get the most description. It felt otherworldly. It felt like I was on the far side of the universe in some unseen and unknown place. I even tried to google images of galaxies to see if I could find the same one. I did find one or two that felt like they could have been it.

Each time I went, I orbited the galaxy several times. With the core aglow, bright starts near me, golden nebula sparkled their way between the spiral arms. It felt as if the galaxy knew I was there. I also had the feeling I wasn't alone. Were there other earths below or an accompaniment of heavenly beings? I could feel God's presence in the fabric of creation. The voice of the Lord sat in my spirit as a counselor for the whole experience.

Trying to remain in the moment was not too far from Jaxon enduring the unlimited presence of Jesus. It reminded me of the young man who tried to endure the light and heat in a Smith Wigglesworth meeting before he crawled out of the room. There are those among us who stumble into more of God than is survivable in the natural yet somehow endure. The secret is to move from glory to glory. These experiences transcend space and time, as God allows access to the reserved part of Him that only walking through fire can unlock. He gives us free access to all of Him, but to get there, are we willing to return the gift, to give Him all of us? The fire always tells.

I kept going back into something that would burn me out for me to take the next trip. Glory to glory takes discipline. It's being thankful for one moment but longing for the next—a continual pursuit. God sees Himself in me and invites me into Himself in these encounters. When I am willing to lose myself in Him, I will discover my supernatural identity. And come out a burning one.

Activation

1. Start as I did with visualization. Imagine the stars. Survey God's beauty and design. Find His presence and connect in wonder.
2. Ask Him to give you a cosmic encounter. Don't try to journal it at first. Enjoy the ride. If it's too intense, remain as long as you can. If you exit the encounter, activate your spirit to go back. Be persistent. If you're having trouble, use the four stages of prayer as a tool to help you ascend.

CHAPTER 5 | CURIOUS WONDERS

Seeds.

I thought I was pulling fuzz off my hoodie sleeves.

After being slightly distracted by it during my friend Eric Gilmour's message, I realized what was happening. I glanced down between my feet, examining the floor, only to find nothing there.

When we went to lunch afterward, I told him that seeds were coming out of my hoodie as he shared. Not knowing what they were, I dropped them onto the ground. The floor was concrete in the little town of Calhoun in northern Georgia. Eric was there doing his School of His Presence. Being friends since bible school days, I wanted to come out and support him and catch up a bit. However, God always seems to be orbiting Him.

Laughing, he says, "You and your wonders, man."

"I know bro, as you spoke, seeds were manifesting. But, when I looked under my seat, where they should've been, they were gone."

At that point, there should've been a small pile.

"It's as if the seed of your message went down into the earth, and the soil itself will never be the same."

Eric is known for the manifestation of miracles and the presence of the Lord when he shares. He's been an encourager of mine in life, ministry, and the deeper things of God for many years. He has a way of grounding you in the endless pleasure of just being with Jesus Himself. In its simplicity, being with Jesus opens up the glory that surrounded His life in your life. He is our focus, the ocean we jump into. But by jumping in, the world of the ocean opens up to us.

Grounded

We are going from the edge of the universe in the last chapter all the way back to the simplicity of the parables in this chapter. We will pause from the gigantic or cosmic type encounters and infuse our journey with some simple, down-to-earth moments. They are no less spectacular, but they show how God moves every day. Don't worry, though, we have plenty of cosmic adventures left on our radar! After we land for a minute, we will take back off.

The Parable of the Seed and the Sower is one of Jesus' most familiar. Many quote it today and rightly so, relate it to the word. That is part of it, but with Jesus, all the parables were about revealing His Kingdom. Revisiting this parable from that perspective one day transformed how I viewed it. Jesus used common things in His day to reveal heavenly mysteries.

He taught them many things by using stories, parables to illustrate spiritual truths, saying: Consider this: There was a farmer who went out to sow *seeds*. As he cast his *seeds*, some fell along the beaten path and the birds came and ate them. Others fell onto gravel that had no topsoil. They quickly shot up, but when the days grew hot, they were scorched and withered because they had insufficient roots. Others fell among the thorns, so when they sprouted, the thorns choked them. But other *seeds* fell on good, rich soil that kept producing a good harvest. Some yielded thirty, some sixty, and some even one hundred times as much as he planted! If you're able to understand this, then you need to respond.

Matthew 13:3-9 TPT

He who has ears, let him hear.

v 9 ESV

The message of the kingdom is the word of God. Hidden within this message is the ability to experience the kingdom. Those who experience it are empowered to reproduce it. Here we see the process of reception.

Recently, the Holy Spirit asked me about my life and the different types of ground the seed—message and reality of the kingdom—fell upon.

"Which soil are you?"

I looked back at my life and realized that I had been all of the soils in different places, times, and seasons.

Now you are ready to hear the explanation of the parable of the sower: What was sown along the path represents the one who listens to the message of the kingdom but doesn't understand it. The Adversary then comes and snatches away what was sown into his heart. The one sown on gravel represents the person who gladly hears the kingdom message, but his experience remains shallow. Shortly after he hears it, troubles and persecutions come because of the kingdom message he received. Then he quickly falls away, for the truth didn't sink deeply into his heart. The one sown among thorns represents one who receives the message, but all of life's busy distractions, his divided heart, and his ambition for wealth result in suffocating the kingdom message and it becomes fruitless. But what was sown on good, rich soil represents the one who hears and fully embraces the message of the kingdom. Their lives bear good fruit— some yield a harvest of thirty, sixty, even one hundred times as much as was sown.

vv 18-23 TPT

In my initial encounter with Jesus, I can see where the seed went really deep, really fast. Later, the Adversary came and almost pulled my roots completely out. My walk became very shallow at times as the world's temptations almost burned up my newly sprouted growth. Some places in my walk yielded amazing fruit and other places none as I relied on my own sufficiency above my relationship with Jesus.

Holy Spirit then asked me, "How did you get here? How are you still in love with Jesus?"

It's as if He answered for me, "You stayed faithful through all the different stages of soil. When the Adversary came, you did not stop. When the ground was rocky, you pushed through. When the heat was intense, you found the living water."

What a new way to look at this ageless passage! Yes, the traditional way of viewing it is equally true, but hidden within are stages of life in the kingdom all of us walk through. The secret is to keep walking, growing, and remaining with Him.

The invitation Jesus gives to "have ears to hear" and respond to the message reveals the hidden layer of meaning. It's not just a spiritual survival parable; it's the fulness of the kingdom and how it grows on the earth. Those who rise through the four stages can grow in any climate, yielding exponential returns of heaven on earth.

"Eyes to see" and "ears to hear" are phrases that Jesus used throughout His ministry to reveal more profound meaning and activate the ones in whom the message takes root.

Seeing what the Lord is doing amid the Adversary's plans, the rocky ground of life, and the blazing sun of tribulation is like a stream flowing in the desert of David seeing God above Goliath. It's the mystery unveiled. It's apprehending heavenly realities in the beauty of daily life. It's the ability to be utterly cosmic and peacefully grounded. It's operating in heavenly realms while doing earthly life well.

Holy Spirit then showed me how some of the curious wonders Allessia and I have experienced were made available through this childlike paradigm.

Why would God cause seeds to grow out of a cotton hoodie? Because the kingdom is transcendent of all earthly reality. He was tying all of this together to make the simple point that He is in outrageous love with us and sends in these kinds of miracles as "I love you's" to us. The majesty within the seed of miracles is the expanse of heavenly dominion. Glimpses of heaven touching earth rewire it according to His image and adopts creation into His family. Besides, cotton (my hoodie) naturally produces seeds, so it did what it was created to do—no different from Aaron's rod budding.

> On the next day Moses went into the tent of the testimony, and behold, the staff of Aaron for the house of Levi had sprouted and put forth buds and produced blossoms, and it bore ripe almonds.
>
> Numbers 17:8 ESV

Coffee Shop Vibrations

Simple chats with a friend about Jesus multiplies the kingdom. It's how we build one another's faith. Sharing testimonies causes the family to burn brightly. *Mystify* and *Mesmerize* have this goal in mind. I am sharing with you the way I would with my wife, a friend, or a congregation.

One such conversation transpired outside Atlanta at a Starbucks when my friend, David Abraham, was in town for a visit. After briefly catching up, our hearts turned to heavenly things.

David suits his namesake as "a man after God's own heart." We often run into each other at gatherings and conferences in pursuit of the majesty of God. He has seen some extraordinary miracles and wonderful salvations in his life through campus ministry, revival, and being a daily witness of Jesus.

Like those trading collectibles from their most recent excursion, we began sharing about the treasures of God we were experiencing in our current seasons. Allessia and I were right in the middle of the cycle of elemental encounters described in *Mystify*. David had been following some of this journey and was eager to hear the stories firsthand.

We were sitting at a long table that could seat nearly 20. The section we were in was near the door of the café. We sat across from each other at front third of the table. A lady quietly worked on both her computer and her iced latte at the far end.

"So, tell me about these experiences," David graciously inquired with eyes full of expectation. In brevity, I walked him through the season up to that point, telling of my house shaking, the wind blowing, and all the incredible stories that happened in Anniston, AL.

As our discussion found its pace, we were already aware of God's presence. Our spiritual senses heightened as we talked about the elements of creation. Soon, the fact we were in a public space surrounded by people faded as the supernatural invaded.

We could feel Him.

Him in our conversation.

Him in Starbucks.

Him in the table?

Our voices raised as our joy, smiles, and the mutual understanding that God was all around us became clear. I could feel His presence pulsating through me, almost like the fine buzzing the day my house shook. Waves of heavenly energy[48] flowed through me.

I am not sure of the exact sequence of what happened next, whether he asked me to pray for him or if I just was inspired to do what I did. Testimonies are trigger points for "what was" to happen again. I could feel a fresh encounter bubbling[49] up by telling the story. I looked down and saw the wood on the table in front of me like a pool of water with ripples flowing from one seat to the other.

"Put your hand on the table," I instructed with a sneaky grin.

Setting my hand down first, it felt like connecting electric currents. Creation, again, was responding to the presence of God and the frequency of the Spirit. The table

[48] *Ruach*, the Hebrew word for Spirit, is often described as life-giving energy or heavenly "breath" of life force. Therefore, using it in this way elevates how we may view the operation of the Person of the Holy Spirit in our present day.
[49] *Nabi* is one of the Hebrew words for *"prophet"* or *"seer"* in the Old Testament, which means to *"bubble up"* or flow forth.

itself was shaking, like the fine vibrations flowing through the structure of my house that day.

David put his hand on the table next. The corners of his mouth and eyelids stretch to capacity as an electric surge shoots up through his hand and up his arm.

"You feel that?"

"Whoa, yeah!" He grins back, leaning back in his chair, hand firmly planted on the table. Eyes locked, we could feel it shaking and vibrating right there in Starbucks. We looked over to the other end to see that the lady was sitting back away from the table. Her drink, half-empty, rippled in the plastic cup.

For the next few minutes, we became children, placing our hands on and off the table, feeling the vibrations. We bent down, looking underneath and back up again. I even put my hand on the concrete floor to see if the whole place was in a rumble. We moved our hands to different spots to feel various degrees of intensity. We even stood up and looked around to see if anyone else noticed.

"The table is vibrating," we said, but those around us didn't comprehend what we meant.

It's seeing the bud of an almond tree—God moving supernaturally in a natural setting that could have any number of natural explanations—electricity, the lady's computer, or the espresso machines. Upon examination, I felt no vibrations on the floor, which would've been impressive to have a coffee grinder powerful enough to shake the concrete foundation. We check not in doubt but to protect the integrity of the encounter.

We exchanged a series of "Wow's" and "Yay God's" as we sat in a coffee shop, sharing about God, as our table shook in His presence.

"But why tho?"

"Seeds growing out of hoodies, tables shaking at Starbucks!"

"You've lost me, Dave."

Don't worry-we are just getting started!

Logic looks for a reason, and reason asks, "why?" Logic and reason aren't negative. They have helped advance the human race. However, they have also caused the supernatural to be viewed as a myth by secularists and deception by cessationists. Many believe God could "sovereignly" do such things, but not in (most of) us experiencing them.

If you were to travel back in time to the world in which the biblical stories took place, you would step into a culture that had an experiential worldview. The natural and spiritual realms were not divided by logic and reason. Instead, interaction with God's realm (heaven) and His realm interacting with theirs (earth) would have been the foundation for their faith.

As adopted sons and daughters of God, we are inheritors of this faith. We recite verses like:

He said to them, "Because of your little faith. For truly, I say to you, if you have faith like a grain of mustard seed, you will say to this mountain,

'Move from here to there,' and it will move, and nothing will be impossible for you."

Matthew 17:20 ESV

Yet, when something natural is moved by the supernatural, we can react in doubt. Often, when people experience the very things written in the bible as proof of God's presence, the religious mindset will actually say that it is not in the bible and label it as demonic. This is "un-metanoia" or thinking from below rather than thinking from above. Such thinking misidentifies what is of God and what is of the devil because it is disconnected and afraid of supernatural experiences. Therefore, they conclude that all supernatural experiences and those who claim them must be "false."

This kind of thinking is divorced from the bible and from who God is. It is His joy for His kids to experience Him. He has seeds of encounters hidden for our joy every day. God is a good Father who loves giving good gifts to His children. He would never give us a snake—something that harms us, instead of bread—something that gives us nourishment.

> What father among you, if his son asks for a fish, will instead of a fish give him a serpent; or if he asks for an egg, will give him a scorpion? If you then, who are evil, know how to give good gifts to your children, how much more will the heavenly Father give the Holy Spirit to those who ask him!"

Luke 11;11-13 ESV

"So why then?"

109

Because God is good, God is fun, God is love, and God is kind. He can do anything, and it's His delight to allow us to experience Him supernaturally.

We were full of wonder, joy, and faith when we left that day. Revelation, insight, and understanding flooded through us, showing us more of Him.

This testimony exercises our faith. What if we find ourselves where we physically need to speak to a mountain and cast it into the sea one day? Now we will have a history with God of experiencing Him move natural things. David killed the lion and the bear[50] before killing Goliath because he was "training for reigning." We saw God do it here, building our faith, so now we believe He will do it again in a bigger way.

Vibrations and Winds in South Africa

Kosie Van der Merwe, a fiery South African friend, read my first book, *The Call for Revivalists*, back in 2012 when it first came out. He reached out to me via social media to thank me for writing the book, which had inspired his walk with the Lord. Over time, we forged a bond of brotherhood, praying for God to extend revival to both of our nations.

Recently, he invited me to share in a Zoom call with his community. Bursting with fire and fresh off the release of *Mystify*, I told them stories from the book, just like with David, and invited them to activate and experience their own encounters.

---

[50] 1 Samuel 17:34-36

On my end, I saw Kosie and some of their faces joined on the call, but I couldn't tell what was happening. Yet, in faith, I knew God was touching these precious saints.

Previously, God moved through Zoom calls in both California and Pakistan. I knew that if He moved then, He would move now. So, whenever I testify about the elements—earth, wind, fire, or water—responding to the presence of God, I am putting myself out there. You can't fake it. God either moves that way, or He doesn't. I simply try to align myself with what He is doing and trust Him to do the rest.

After I prayed for fresh fire to fall on them and that they would experience God in an elemental way, I asked Kosie what was happening. He said people felt the wind blowing and vibrations. Some had heatwaves go through their bodies, and others experienced shakings. There was even a testimony of body temperature dropping as the wind blew. It was hot, and their windows were shut so they could hear the call, making the room stuffy. As the wind of God blew in, the room cooled down and lowered their body temperature. Whether a heatwave or a cool breeze, God moved according to the environment of each participant.[51]

From a coffee shop in Atlanta to a community in South Africa, the winds and vibrations flow across the globe. What will it look like when the earth is covered in His glory? It will look like a supernatural family operating in the fullness of creation. Seeds grow in gardens. The Garden in Eden is the blueprint for

---

[51] Testimony video of winds blowing in South Africa
https://youtu.be/XKJzBKDaVBQ (sacn qr code)

creation. Through these creative encounters, God is revealing the essence of the kingdom. He always has and always will move like this. All that's needed is eyes to see and ears to hear. Then our hearts will perceive!

Activation

1. Ask God to show where He has placed seeds in your life. Note their stages of growth and ask Holy Spirit to water and nourish them into fruition.
2. God has no boundaries, whether in Atlanta or South Africa or any other place in the world. He can touch you right now reading this. A book is not different from a Zoom call or sharing a testimony at a live event. Allow these stories to inspire you. Ask God to move through the elements of creation around you now. Pray through this activation:
   a. Papa, can I feel your wind?
   b. Papa, can I feel your fire?
   c. Papa, can I feel your rain?
   d. Papa, can I feel your vibration?

CHAPTER 6 | BENDING REALITY

The walls of the thatched church seemed to warp as waves of heavenly glory moved around us like a whirlpool. We were way out in the middle of the bush in Uganda, Africa. The pastor spun like a top as I prayed for him with my finger placed lightly in the center of his back.

I looked over to Jaxon—his eyes glazed with eternity. A jolt of fire picked up the one he laid his hands on as they flew through the air, banked to the left, and bounced off the walls. The grassy bamboo walls should have collapsed upon impact. Instead, they slowed gravity, redirecting the energy of the worshipper down as she rolled onto the dirt floor and into ecstatic joy, laughter, and electric vibrations.

"What in the world is going on?" I asked.

It was as if reality itself was bending in the presence of the King of Majesty. I had heard only one story like this before, a story so "out there" that finding myself in the middle of a similar situation caught me by surprise. To this day, this is the most supernatural, wild, and extravagant encounter I have ever witnessed. I have tried to describe it less than a handful of times, falling short on each one. Hopefully, the 20 years since as given me the grace and the language to share it with you. However, when Jaxon and I reminisce about that day, earthly definitions fall short every time.

How Did We Get Here?

Jaxon and I were in each other's weddings in 2001. With one semester of ministry school left, we dreamed of going to Africa after graduation to work with his family's ministry there. He and Avi had gone the previous summer and witnessed many miracles, which only whet our appetite to leap onto the mission field.

At the time, we were avid David Hogan fans. He is a missionary to Mexico who operates in astonishing signs and wonders. Since the 1970s, his ministry team has seen recreative miracles, multiplying food, countless healings, and over 500 resurrections. One of David's teachings back then was "Faith to Raise the Dead." It went viral VHS style before there was such a thing on the internet. He shared it at BRSM, which was already in a state of intense revival. However, they weren't experiencing the kind of miracles David talked about. This was a couple of years before I arrived on campus, but by the time I became a student, the stories he told became the stuff of legend.

He would often minister in cities along the Gulf Coast. Small groups of us would cram into vehicles of all sizes and caravan over to hear him speak. The meetings would go late into the night as the Spirit of God moved. We would stay as long as we could before trying to make it back to class the next day, even stopping at rest areas at midnight to honor curfew before hitting the road again at 5:00 am.

When it came to Hogan stories, if one of us heard a new one, we would wait till all of our mates were gathered to share it in dramatic fashion. Jaxon was a storyteller and would reanimate the details with precision and fire.

We heard about a guy named Mike who lived in the upper Midwest that compiled VHS tapes of Hogan messages and would send you a box full for a donation. So, we ordered one, which arrived full of tapes and CDs. It was like Christmas morning for us. As we made our way through the messages, story after story of incredible encounters boosted our walk with Jesus and increased our expectations.

As we unearthed the treasures in this box, we discovered a story of God bending the law of physics. It was one of those that both sticks out when you first hear it and sticks with you for life. We had no idea that stewarding this testimony well would set us up to have a story to tell of our own.

David Hogan and his team heard of an unreached village high on a mountaintop. After hiking all day, they found only four people in the village. There were twice as many people in their party, but the numbers did not matter. They were souls who needed a Savior. Hogan noted that he preaches with the same intensity, whether four or thousands.

Although I have listened to this story multiple times, it has been years since I've heard it in detail. I probably have it somewhere, on some CD or VHS, but it would take some time to rediscover it. The specifics of what happens next are blurry and just as hard to articulate as our own story. But I'll do my best here to recall it from memory.

After David finished preaching, the glory of God showed up. Suddenly, it was as if reality began to warp. They felt the weighty glory, but it seemed to affect the atmosphere. One of the men lost his bearings during the encounter and fell to the ground…but he bounced off it like a trampoline…and floated into the air!

God is the God of the impossible, for He made the earth and all it contains (Ps 24), so bending the rules of that which He created is not challenging to Him. He can cause the mountains and hills to change form or shape, jump into the sea, or flatten into a highway (Is 40, Mk 11). He can even change their properties.

> The mountains melt like wax at the presence of the LORD, before the Lord of all the earth.

> Psalm 97:5 Berean

As I edited this story, I had some random music playing in the background. Suddenly, I hear, "Every valley will be raised up, every mountain will be laid low." It's a lyric from the song "Lion,"[52] by Elevation Worship

---

[52] Elevation Worship, "Lion" featuring Brandon Lake and Chris Brown: https://youtu.be/2go_dOJVwc4 (scan qr code)

with Brandon Lake and Chris Brown. What appears to be random are often divine coincidences the Lord gives us to let us know we are surrounded by His guidance and His gaze, leading us in the direction He has for us. Take a moment to scan the link and listen. Allow Him to "elevate" your perception of all that is possible in Him!

It would be easy to claim that using Psalm 97 as a scriptural reference takes it out of context but consider what the biblical author was saying. He used metaphor to describe just how powerful Yahweh is because metaphor is a way of pulling the mind out of earthly realities (limitations) into heavenly thinking (limitlessness). It paints a picture of just how big God is, one that was previously painted at Mt. Saini, which is an obvious inspiration for this Psalm (Exodus 19:18). In seeing Him this way, the metaphor becomes obtainable, revealing that God can move in these majestic ways "literally" on your behalf. Sometimes our literal reality is below what He can "literally" do. Metaphors are used in Scripture to break this restriction and merge what we deem as literal into His reality.

> The Lord reigns, let the earth be glad; let the distant shores rejoice.
>
> Clouds and thick darkness surround him; righteousness and justice are the foundation of his throne.
>
> Fire goes before him and consumes his foes on every side.
>
> His lightning lights up the world; the earth sees and trembles.

The mountains melt like wax before the Lord, before the Lord of all the earth.

The heavens proclaim his righteousness, and all peoples see his glory.

Psalm 97 ESV

The surrounding verses of this have notes of Apocalyptic Literature. As introduced earlier, this is a form of literary genre in the bible that shows what happens when everything is "unveiled," and the Creator shows up. It is always accompanied by elemental effects, as you can see in the verses:

- The "Earth" rejoices at His appearance (v1).
- "Clouds" cover His throne (v2)—Elemental encounters accompanying His throne, as in Ezekiel. Clouds are atmospheric and include the air and the wind.
- "Fire" is always present when He is (v3).
- "Lightning" again signifies His appearing and is a dazzling display of His presence (v4a).
- The "Earth sees." The earth knows who He is and reacts to Him (v4b). Likewise, the earth reacts to His presence in His family—us.
- And "Trembles," another example of the earth shaking and vibrating in the magnitude of His glory (v4c).
- "Mountains" transform (v5). Physics bend according to His will.
- "Heavens" respond to earth (v6)—A heaven and earth interaction, revealing His glory. Whenever these encounters occur, they are accompanying His presence (His throne), causing all the earth

118

(creation) and people (His family) to rejoice and glorify Him.

When I wrote *Mystify*, I didn't know about the pattern of elemental encounters accompanying God's presence and throne. But the more I studied to learn about my encounters and examine the biblical record, I found that they weren't just connected to biblical principles but were a demarcation of His appearing and unveiling. Now, with "eyes to see and ears to hear," the apocalyptic design rises to the surface in other familiar passages. Holy Spirit is God, and in His coming on the Day of Pentecost, the "people" were immersed in the encounter (the encounter swallowed them up). The fire then is interconnected to fire mentioned in other verses within this literary context. There is a flow from prophetic psalms, such as this one, the transfiguration of Jesus, to the baptism of the Spirit, to God moving through the elements today. Peter even quotes Joel in reference to this:

> This is what I will do in the last days—I will pour out my Spirit on everybody and cause your sons and daughters to prophesy, and your young men will see visions, and your old men will experience dreams *from God*. The Holy Spirit will come upon all my servants, men and women alike, and they will prophesy. I will reveal startling signs and wonders in the sky above and mighty miracles on the earth below. Blood and fire and pillars of cloud will appear. For the sun will be turned dark and the moon blood-red before that great and awesome appearance of the

day of the Lord. But everyone who calls on the name of the Lord will be saved.

Acts 2:17-22 TPT

His description, recognized by the Apostle Peter as the moment of fulfillment, is a detail of all of heaven—the heavens (cosmos) and the earth—being affected by the people of the Spirit in the same way as the presence of the Lord affects the physical realm in apocalyptic literature. Why? Because He Himself is with them. Pentecost is Joel fulfilled. It spirals throughout the New Testament, church history, and today.

Unfortunately, apocalyptic literature is often misunderstood today. It's so majestic that many assume it's unattainable. Others misidentify miracles associated with heavenly appearances and view anything elemental as witchcraft. The enemy counterfeits supernatural experiences in the elements to discredit when God genuinely moves through them—as found in apocalyptic literature. He tries to use manipulation to generate a false demonstration of that which the King and His family naturally walk in.

Remember, Satan does have power in the second heaven, and he can use that to manipulate the elements. But just because he does a bad copy it doesn't mean that someone experiencing God move in the elements of creation is automatically witchcraft. Witchcraft is counterfeit spiritual authority used to manipulate and control. It never leads to Jesus; it misleads things about Him. False encounters do not erase the genuine. However, genuine encounters expose that which is false and brings the one experiencing it closer to Jesus.

120

Before the digital age, there were bootleg copies of new movies. However, one could immediately tell if it was genuine as it was clearly a copy of a copy. It loses quality the further it gets from the source. Drink from the Source, Jesus Himself, and your life will be filled with genuine miracles that no false encounter could survive.

The point of apocalyptic literature is that the laws of the earth, the heavens, and the elements all bend when He comes. The ground shakes before him, the hills melt like wax, and we could go on and on with other biblical descriptions. There is so much biblical precedent for God moving like this that it wouldn't fit in this book.

When He comes, these things happen. If they aren't happening, is it Him? We should start to consider genuine encounters from the reverse perspective. God is supernatural by default. If it's not supernatural, it is disconnected from the God of the bible. The only supernatural warnings in there were to show the enemy also has power, not that all supernatural experiences were from the enemy. Again, he cannot create; he can only produce counterfeit or perverted copies.

The **true marks** of an apostle—**signs, wonders, and miracles**—were performed among you with great perseverance.

2 Corinthians 12:12 Berean *emphasis mine*

Page after page in the New Testament, Jesus is performing miracles. Page after page in the bible, the wind blows, fire falls, the earth shakes, and the heavens open up as God touches His people. Of course, the enemy doesn't want this, so if he can't trick you with fakes, he'll say it's all fake. Remember, counterfeit money doesn't make all money counterfeit.

Jesus supernaturally transformed the earth with every step, every touch, and every word. Jesus in His people will be a supernatural display of love and power. If the waters can solidify to hold His weight, the mountains can melt...

The word David Hogan used to describe what was happening in that mountain-transforming encounter was "Jello." It was as if the ground, the trees, even the rocks had the buoyancy of Jello (a fruity gelatin dessert). They grabbed hold of the tree trunks to keep themselves both upright. As the encounter intensified, colors swirled, speech slurred, and things got loopy. They thought they had been in the glory for 15 minutes, but when they looked at their watches, four hours had passed. All the laws of physics bent around them in a spectacular display as heaven came down on a remote mountain. A hill became a volcano in the Spirit, erupting with the fire of God.

Uganda

Now, we will leap back from a remote mountain in Latin America to our little village in Uganda. The similarities are both striking and tender. Heaven was touching earth to no fanfare. Jesus chose to touch two small groups of people gathered with one agenda, "to know Jesus and make Him known."

We were somewhere, nowhere no one could find. Jaxon and I had arrived three weeks prior, with our new brides and ministry school diplomas. The stories from

Hogan and others during our time in training inspired an adventurous spirit within us. We longed to forge our own pathways in untouched areas for the Gospel. While I was a freshman on African soil, we did have missionary experience under our belts. Two summers before, I went with my home church to Honduras, whereas Jaxon's dad had been a missionary in Uganda for over twenty years, so he'd been there many times. When they were there the year before, they even saw two babies raised from the dead, one for which Jaxon and Avi personally prayed. Jaxon said that when the mother placed the lifeless body in his hands, it was stiff and had the odor of a dead animal. He lifted the little body in the air to the Lord Jesus and thanked God for resurrection life. Then he handed the child back to the mom, alive and moving. This only added fuel to our fire and raised the bar of expectancy to extreme levels. We knew God would do amazing things again this year.

Armed with M&M's

Feet on the ground, our hearts were bursting for miracles. Then, on only the second day, my wife's eyes turned to tears as Jaxon, his dad, and I loaded up the Toyota Hilux and headed west to Ft. Portal, a city in the foothills of the Rwenzori mountains on the border of the DRC (Democratic Republic of the Congo). She cried because we had yet to be apart in our 11 months of marriage. And she cried because we were going into an area that had recently been subject to terroristic activities by the LRA.

Our dreams of heroism now faced the reality of leaving our spouses behind and going into danger zones.

Thrills of excitement coupled with the complexities of coming face to face with life-threatening situations. It's one thing to hear a testimony about those who've come through such trials. It's another to be in the truck, not knowing if a terror cell is waiting around the corner. At the tender age of 22, our perceived bravery was about to be tested with fire.

As we winded our way through the high mountain pass that was sometimes only as wide as a single vehicle with a two-thousand-foot drop-off to one side, we found ourselves stuck behind a truck full of Ugandan soldiers. They laughed and teased as they pointed their AK-47s at the vehicle full of mzungus behind them. Jaxon and I looked at each other like "what did we get ourselves into?" We were a long way from sitting on our couch watching testimonies of people in places like this, surviving experiences like this, and reciting, "Yeah, we can take it." But such is the zeal of young men.

His dad didn't miss a beat. He told Jaxon to hand him the giant bag of M&M's from the glove compartment. Sticking his right arm out the window, he began whistling to get their attention while his left hand carefully navigated the steering wheel of the right-hand drive truck, preventing us from sliding off the dirt road into the valley below. When they finally acknowledged, he tossed the king-sized bag of candy up to them, followed by loud cheers. Big smiles ran across their faces as they shared in their newfound delights. They waved, thanking us for their gift. Tension turned to peace through the wisdom and foresight of Jaxon's dad bringing a bag of candy for moments such as this.

We now had an armed escort as we ventured further through the mountains above the Semliki River valley. We quickly discovered the value of finding Jesus in the normal—sweets—and how He can use that to open up doors (a way through) and shut doors (keep us safe). Feet on the ground, I expected miracles right away, but lessons like this would pave the way for them.

The Upper Room

Three weeks later, I rose early at our compound to go upstairs to an empty room to spend time in God's Presence. My Walkman played a mix of my favorite worship songs at the time. My zeal was steady but met with the reality of life on the mission field. It was epic. It was trying. Full of joy, full of challenge. The miracles I had dreamed about had yet to happen. Yes, God had already moved and touched people. I preached my first open-air crusade with my best friend and our wives. These were very precious and valuable to me. But I had yet to see the miracles I'd envisioned.

Was it me? Had I disappointed the Lord? Was I not spending enough time with Him? These were all questions I brought before my Father as the day outside brightened. Before long, I found myself lost in His embrace with Michael W. Smith's "Let it Rain" on repeat. My self-analyzations, trivial as they were, evaporated in adoration. Charged with renewed focus, I skipped forward to Freddie Haylor's "Celestial Odyssey." As I listened and visualized the encounter, I was unaware that we were on a collision course for heaven to come to us.

With it now nearly 7:00 am, I headed downstairs to help load up the van for the day's journey and, yet again, kiss my wife goodbye, although she did go on almost every other crusade. This would be a one-vehicle trek as we were only staying the night—Jaxon, me, and a couple of brothers.

About two hours after we had left the city, we turned off A109, the main highway that connected Kampala to Kenya onto a small, bumpy dirt road that divided the rice fields. I thought that we must be getting close, only to quickly realize that the bumps would be with me for the next hour. "It's just up ahead" simply means that you are closer than when you left, I had come to find out in my ETA inquiries.

The Unknown Martyr

We arrived even later than I expected, somewhere between mid-bump as my arm wore out the handle above the window. As we rounded the front of the white building that would be our home for the night, it was bigger than it appeared. Two wings extended from the main hall to the back, forming a U shape.

As the sliding door of the small van clanged to a stop, a man greeted us:

"Hi, welcome. We are so glad you're here."

I thought, "this is nice, a warm welcome after a long journey," without warning of what he was about to say next!

"The last missionary who was here was martyred right there." A big smile gleamed across his face as he pointed to the spot.

"We knew that God would send someone else, and that devil could not stop what Jesus wants to do."

An inhale.

"And here you are!"

"So, welcome, this way."

An exhale.

"Wait!" "WHAT?" My thoughts turned into words as Jaxon followed with a "Whoa—Really?"

"Yes, he died right here. He was martyred," he said as he walked around gesturing, showing us the position this saint's body was in as he gave his life for the gospel.

He continued without missing a beat...

"Watch out for the rice," as it was spread out across the concrete, drying in the sun. It would later be part of our dinner as small pebbles that had been swept up with the granules cracked in our teeth as we chewed.

"This way, I'll show you to your room."

We humbly followed, locking eyes, thinking, "Now, what did we get ourselves into?"

Nervous energy flowed as we pondered, "do we want to ask for more details or just roll with it?" I think we ended up doing a little of both. After all, we were here. We drove all this way to share with these people. A heavy price had been paid, and Heaven sent us in honor of the sacrifice. It was not an offer to refuse but a privilege to embrace.

Slightly in shock, we followed him into the courtyard between the wings of the building. Smokey fires were going as the locals prepared big meal to follow the church meeting. There were doors on both sides leading into small rooms like an old roadside motel in the USA.

Jaxon squeezed his six-foot-plus frame through the narrow doorway. A single-person cot snuggled against the wall on the left side of the tiny room with a makeshift mosquito net above attached via ladies underclothing and a one-square-foot table next to it. Beneath it was a hen, sitting on her eggs. My frame back then was relatively skinny. However, Jaxon was tall with a burly stature. Somehow, both of us would have to lie side-by-side that night on a cot designed for a small African frame. Little did we know, but the hen would become the infamous snoring chicken, keeping us much further from sleep than we already would be well after midnight. We were thankful though; this was the nice room—it had a bed.

I walked back out into the sunshine to see everyone smiling, singing, and doing life in the joy of the Lord, and I thought that today was very nearly perfect. How in the world did we get here? We had no idea that all of the things we had experienced on the continent up to this point were a shadow of things to come. The supernatural provision and protection via a bag of M&M's were necessary for us to not crumble under the weight of being the very next missionaries to visit a place where the last one was martyred for his faith. We also wouldn't have known how to value his blood if we had not faced life-threatening circumstances and walked right through them.

This place was the home of these precious believers. Sometimes, fleeing is the only option, but they chose to stay. When persecution rang at the door, they stood their ground, happily worshipping the Lord with the little they had. We knew we had been sent to kings and queens.

The Glory Comes

Time got blurry as this was our only plan for the rest of the day. We did have a goal to be done before nightfall, though, as we literally wouldn't be able to see anything. There were no outdoor lights. Our makeshift sound system was just a keyboard and mic running off a generator.

We tag-team preached that evening, pouring our heart and soul into the message. Together, we called the people up for a time of prayer, impartation, and going after God for more of Him. As we began to pray, the atmosphere already rich with presence began to combust as Holy Spirit filled not only the church but also the grounds. As we laid hands on the people, the manifestations quickly exceeded what we had ever experienced.

I cannot quote Romans 8:19 enough because when heaven comes like this, all natural laws and physical properties give way to the One who created them. They bend and flex according to His will, His Person, His divine majesty. "All creation groans for the sons and daughters of God to be revealed." The revelation of kingdom family is an ignition point for Father, Son, and Spirit to harmonize with those created in Their image, triggering an outlet of praise from creation itself and causing it to come alive as always intended.

Really, it had nothing to do with us. I mean, yes, God sent us and chose us to be there, but all we could do was ride the wave of glory flowing from heaven to earth as it filled our hearts, the church, and all the surrounding life. The church walls seemed to bend and move with the navigation of the Spirit. The trees were buzzing with heavenly energy. We could see air currents like twirls and whisps dance around the people as fiery bursts of color moved within and without.

Many began to lift their voices in tongues to a level I had not seen before. It was loud and fervent as they released the declarations of heaven with undaunted authority and tone.

Trying to capture, retain, appreciate, and recite all that was happening was like being tossed around by an ocean wave. The pastor who was helping us to pray began to realize the amplitude of what was upon us and stopped to glean at the opening of heaven's gaze. I went over to pray for him, and it was as if rotational power spiraled out of me. I could feel it flowing from its Godly origin through my being into his. He leaned over and succumbed to glory. My finger touched the middle of his back, and he began to spin around faster than humanly possible, almost like Taz in an Animaniacs cartoon. He physically animated what I spiritually felt.

Jaxon prayed for a lady to my left, she went up into the air in a backward motion away from him. Next, she veered to the left and floated into the grassy barrier, which absorbed her momentum, sending ripples down the walls like the CG in a Matrix movie, and set her gently on the ground again.

Nothing was as it should have been. Heaven was rearranging molecules as the Creator's family rejoiced in His presence. I had no idea if we worshipped for an hour or several. Our watches didn't even make sense as time seemed irrelevant. God kissed the bloodstained earth of one of His persecuted churches, and we were caught in the crossfire of His infinite power. Other things were happening that I still have no language for, nor could any description merit their splendor.

People were all over the ground—a combination of bare dirt and selectively placed mats. The weighty, wobbly glory hit everyone as simple human movements carried the flare of Pentecostalism, unleashing a wave of holy laughter as they groaned, cried, sang, and giggled.

Finding a moment of clarity and motor function, Jaxon, the pastor, and I exited the less than 500 sq ft space to fill our bellies with freshly warmed beans and rice. As we sank our fingers into the hot meal and tried our best to make them forks, a holy satisfaction hit our spirits. The sun was low with people scattered about the grounds, lost in the wonders of God, and we asked ourselves one more time, "How did we get here?"

What do we make of this?

As you read, so much time, trial, and life went into this encounter that it's no surprise God chose to move this way. My heart's cry for something miraculous on the mission field was not only checked but also elevated to unfathomable levels. It's easy to mock something someone hasn't paid the price for, but in knowing the price, it's easy to forgive those who devalue the cost, understanding that the heavenly rewards surpass all and that it's worth it when only a few.

Activation

1. Ask Holy Spirit to show you any limitations that may be present in your thinking about what is possible to experience in Him.
2. Ask God to show you His power in creation: the trees, the sky, the wind, the grass.
3. Ask Him to touch you in a new and tangible way.

CHAPTER 7 | HEAVENLY PORTALS

Buzz.

Pop

Flash.

A jolt of electricity arched from Allessia's back to the wall with all the dazzle of a Sci-fi movie as she finished telling about a portal she encountered the night before.

"What was that?"

"Whoa!"

"Did you hear that?"

"Yes, I saw it to."

We all responded in various ways as a beam of light flashed light a lightning bolt and crackled like a power surge.

"Did everyone hear it?"

"Yes, it was loud."

"Can you believe that just happened?"

Our crew smiled ear-to-ear with excitement, saying, "We're keeping our shoes by the bed, so if another one opens up tonight, we can all go!"

As she shared, our faith met the moment of testimony, heaven opened before us with this manifestation of shekinah electricity, both recreating and solidifying her account. As hearts respond to heaven touching earth, His heart opens up a new place of discovery for those who believe. Some describe these openings as portals or gateways—places where heaven and earth are noticeably one.

Next, with our bellies full of breakfast and our hearts full of wonder, we were ready to tackle the day.

Baptism of Love

I used to think, "Portals! Who needs them?" As far as I was concerned, heaven was always open. Such was the case when a group of believers in one of churches we attended years ago began talking about a specific spot in the building that seemed to carry the manifest glory of God. "Why do they feel like they have to go stand in that spot?" I thought to myself. Expectation filled the air as different ones could feel the atmosphere change as they would step in and out of it.

I was no stranger to extravagant expressions or peculiar manifestations. Yet, this stretched my mind. Nonetheless, I wasn't about to miss an opportunity to experience God in a brand-new way—even if my mind had objections.

I knew these people. We did life together both inside and outside the church. We were a small, yet dedicated group of believers.

In fact, I found my first baptism of love experience in this church family. Our Pastors, Greg and Nancey Tankersley, carried the heart of the Father in a way that I had never seen before. Our church was even called, The Father's House. I would not know the Lord as I do or be where I am today without my time there.

Before then, in the mid 2000s, I was a really on-fire orphan for God. I burned for him and loved Him with all my heart, even preaching and seeing revival sparks from meeting to meeting, but I didn't know my identity in him. So during that time, finding a church home was difficult. I went from place to place and would leave very frustrated, feeling like they "weren't on fire enough" and didn't understand the spirit as I did. I was in the second half of my 20s and, in my inexperience, thought myself an expert.

I had been schooled at the Brownsville Revival, something I cherished deeply but also something I found my identity in. And, if someone or some church crossed this (which unknowingly challenged my identity), I'd leave (run away) because they weren't spiritual enough (they had a different piece of God that I needed but was too scared to let part of me go in order to receive it).

This circle continued for two years until, in 2006, I walked into The Father's House. When worship started,

I immediately went through my mental spiritual grading system and again found them lacking—not knowing it was I who was in lack.

Suddenly, His still small voice whispered to me, "Are you here for them or me?"

I was arrested on the spot as conviction pulled me further into His words. My heart confessed its void as I realized that I had been projecting my own internal lack of love onto unsuspecting fellow believers, making them the bad guy for my internal insufficiencies.

I turned toward the wall, took my attention off them, and gave Jesus the full gaze of my eyes, ears, and heart. I forgot about my surroundings and got lost in Him. I cascaded into pools of love. My tank went from empty to overflowing. As I poured my heart out; His loved flowed in, resetting my love for myself and His people. Worship seemed to end too quickly, although over 45 minutes had passed. As I turned towards the room, I found that I loved them all. My eyes now saw them the way He sees them. I no longer saw where they lacked but how they were full. They were rich, each one a unique part of Papa's heart.

My heart tenderized, and the walls in my mind preventing the exposure of my deficiencies came crumbling down. I knew that in my imperfection, His love made me perfect. And in their imperfection, His love covers and fills them with His perfection. They were the same as they were before worship began when I was cynical, but now I couldn't help but care for each one. I was no longer offended by who they weren't or what they did or did not believe. Rather, I celebrated who they were and looked forward to finding the point of connection.

I wouldn't discover the term that today describes my life message, "kingdom family," for nearly a decade later, but I found a family in this house, my Father's House. I would learn what it was like to become a son to Papa Greg and Mama Nancy. Love and family moved me beyond my black and white mentality and superiority complex in spiritual matters. These things blinded me to the beautiful people right in front of me. I can now celebrate differences, agree to disagree, and be content. Common ground isn't "sloppy agape," saying that any belief system goes. It is a kingdom family that doesn't divide over differences but gathers in His presence, knowing that we are all imperfect, all see in part, and if we stay connected to one another. He won't leave us alone; He will guide us as we grow further in the truth, knowledge, and understanding of Him. Holy Spirit gels us in oneness with all knowledge, insight, and peace.

My baptism of love was vital for me to get out of the doldrums I had created around myself for those two years and begin to move into the next stage of growth God had for me. It also empowered me not to walk right out the back door when people started talking about portals. Instead, I jumped out of my seat and ran up to the front where this "so-called" portal was. The moment I did, I walked right into a hotspot of glory. I could feel that tangible difference of His radiating presence. I looked back at the people and laughed as I announced, "You can totally feel it." Others ran up and stood in it. Some fell to the ground under the weight of His glory, others were submerged in uncontrollable joy.

Before this, I didn't really have a grid for portals as I felt people missed Jesus in the room and simply being present with us all the time. I thought some chased things like this and lost sight of Him. While that can happen to any of us, if the encounter is from Him, it will always lead us back to Him. Trust me, the giggles, the change on people's faces (including my own), and the presence we felt that day only left us all more in love with Jesus.

A Portal describes a place like Jacob's dream where heaven touches earth (Genesis 28). It's not a theology thing but a word choice in the natural about what's happening in the spirit. Think about turning on a water faucet as heaven coming down in a particular place or a gateway from one room or place to the next. It's like a transporter beam like in Star Trek—where crew members would stand in a circle of light that would engulf their bodies and send them to the planets below. Later, Jesus reveals that He was the ladder in Jacob's dream, with angels moving back and forth between heaven and earth. In Him, we can go anywhere, any place, and any time.

> I prophesy to you eternal truth: From now on, you all will see an open heaven and gaze upon the Son of Man like a stairway reaching into the sky with the messengers of God climbing up and down upon him!

> John 1:51 TPT

"Portal" is simply a word used today to describe encounters like this. I don't go looking for portals. I go looking for Jesus and bump into experiences like this along the way. And if I go looking for Jesus and the Spirit leads me to a place where there is a portal of His glory, then that's where I'm going. He guides my gaze—the prism through which all things are clearly seen.

Birmingham Tent Revival 2019

Randy Clark joined Leif Hetland at the third Birmingham Tent Revival in 2019, returning after a two-year hiatus with the first one in 2016. The second followed in 2017, the same tent revival I mentioned in *Mystify,* where the pictures[53] of the cosmos were taken that showed heaven shining through the tent canopy (like a portal). The pictures and the encounter are rich in our history, both for the team at Arise Birmingham (the church that hosted the event) and for Global Mission Awareness (Leif's Ministry). But, on the other hand, Randy Clark had no idea, which makes the next part of this story all the more interesting—er., out of this world.

On the first night of the revival, Randy began to share some unusual supernatural testimonies after a passionate worship set with our friend, Jake Mathenia. First, he told how one time he was dealing with a slipped disk and was struggling to sleep. Then, in a meeting in a different city, a man saw Randy's skeletal system in a vision. A Voice (Holy Spirit) told him to push the slipped disk back in. When Randy woke up in the morning, all the pain was gone. He used that story to set us up for the next so we could see beyond natural sight and how it can impact the earthly realm.

Next, he proceeds to tell us that he doesn't often talk about this but that he believed there was a portal here on

---

[53] YouTube Video about the BHM Tent Revival 2017 showing the cosmos shining in the tent canopy: https://youtu.be/skhsdhRsiYk (scan qr code) 

this property. But, again, he did not have a clue about the history of the property, its connection to revival, or the heavenly portal captured in pictures just two years ago. He framed this by telling us about portals that were visibly seen in different countries.

The first story was about a man sticking his hands into a portal and pulling them back out to see that they were covered in gold dust. Other times he would pull them out, and they would be covered in oil. Gold and oil are substances often connected in Scripture to heaven and presence. Inside the portal, it looked like the cosmos! Like it was in another dimension with small stars and galaxies. When the man put his hands in it, he could move the stars around as they were illuminated with light. He then reveals he feels a portal will open up here for healing, using the story portal containing the cosmos to illustrate it.

We were all stunned as he said this. It added clarity to the "why" of the pictures from last time, confirmation that God was in it, and application for the future.

Randy is a master teacher and activator. He holds a Doctor of Divinity and a Doctor of Theology. However, his academic prowess adds to his fire rather than subtracting from it. He's not just recalling a wonder; he's teaching us how to steward a portal—open heaven.

What may look like foolishness—a man pushing Randy's disk back in place in thin air—became an "act of obedience" that manifested a result. Now, he's showing that there is more to seeing a vision. You can interact with it in your physical body. As heaven increases all around you, it often becomes hard to tell which is which, as we discovered from Paul's trip to heaven.

> Someone I'm acquainted with, who is in union with Christ, was swept away fourteen years ago in an ecstatic experience. He was taken into the third heaven, but I'm not sure if he was in his body or out of his body—only God knows. And I know that this man (again, I'm not sure if he was still in his body or taken out of his body—God knows) was caught up in an ecstatic experience and brought into paradise, where he overheard many wondrous and inexpressible secrets that were so sacred that no mortal is permitted to repeat them.

> 2 Corinthians 12:2-4 TPT

Randy then talks about the next portal, which manifested in Russia. It appeared in the home of a man who had an apostolic ministry and led thousands of people to the Lord. It stayed there for over a year. He could see it, and it felt like energy when he put his hands in. Then, after he could no longer see it, for another year, he could go over there, put his hands where it had been, and still feel it. The final stories are of Randy's personal experience with portals. I'll recount his words from the video linked below.[54]

> My daughter and son-in-law were with me in England. We started to pray, and to the left, about the size of a smaller trampoline was a

---

[54] Video of the Birmingham Tent Revival 2019 with Randy Clark sharing about heavenly portals: https://youtu.be/dTgJiyqmnal

portal. I call it a portal; I don't know how else to explain it. Anybody who got close to that spot fell out in the spirit. People would come over out of curiosity, get too close, and fall in.

We had the same thing happen in Medellin, Columbia. A portal opened up; it was amongst kids. They got close to it [and] they'd just fall in. They'd start laughing and get really, really impacted.

Although we didn't see it at the Father's House, this is exactly what happened to us. I believe the other portal stories reveal what they look like in the spirit. The first gentleman was able to see it with his eyes.

Rita's House

We were starstruck at the connection between the portal and cosmic pictures as we retired to Rita's house for the evening. Allessia and I had stayed here before on our trips to Birmingham. She lives on top of a mountain. Her home looks like something out of the Cotswold's, which is befitting, given the city's name. I often joked that we'd move here if we ever moved to Birmingham. Not easy to get to and hard to find, it was a hidden gem of glory. Rita knows how to pray and has stories cataloged in the "mind-blowing" section and would vanquish all the space I have left in the pages of this book if I were to attempt to share them here. At the time, she was the chief intercessor for Leif Hetland Ministries and had accompanied him on many mission trips. We call her Mama Rita as she cares for our bodies and soul every time we see her.

She informed Allessia that there was a portal in her house earlier that day, with no notion of what Randy would talk about in his message. My wife, with eager expectation, was ready to find out where it was. I was feeling sick to my stomach and ready for bed. We were staying in the master suite. The rest of the team—Kayleigh, Hayley, Katchig, and Elise shared rooms at the front of the house.

After an hour of debriefing and downtime, we made our way to our chamber. It was late, and I found myself tired yet unable to sleep. Allessia in contrast was giddy, ready to encounter God, and had discovered that the bed had a built-in massager. As the night pressed on, Allessia fell asleep as I finally made my way to bed, having found some relief from indigestion. The series of events that follow are best told by Allessia, as a heavenly encounter awakens her. On the contrary, I didn't know what was going on, flowing in and out of REM during the experience.

She begins by backing up a bit and sharing earlier events from her perspective. They are key to grasping the prophetic significance of why and how God was moving and how it ties into the weekend.

When we arrived at the Tent Revival, I shared with Rita how I was reading *Bending Time* by Dan McCullum and how it raised my expectations for God to move outside of time. A few minutes later, the hands on my wristwatch went haywire, spinning around in different directions. I laughed with a beaming smile as my gaze turned to heaven, "You're doing it again,

Lord." On several previous occasions, my watch did this just as God was either moving or about to. That night, my expectation for the meeting grew as I knew Heaven was certainly up to something.

Our conversation turned to portals as we were discussing prayer before the services began. Mama Rita proceeded to tell me that there was a portal on the property where the Tent Revival was taking place. Playfully, I asked her to let me discern where it was located. Later that evening, Randy Clark was teaching at the event and started talking about the portal of healing he felt was on the property! After the service, she came over to me and told me she also had a portal in her home, where we were staying that evening. I was very expectant because God was clearly speaking to me about access!

As I was getting the bed ready, I discovered that it had a massage function. So I absolutely tested it out before bed and then went to sleep.

Suddenly, in the early morning hours, I woke up with the bed shaking. I looked over to Dave, and he was sound asleep. The bed was violently shaking as if a storm were passing through. The wall itself was vibrating, and there was a sound that I can only describe as "many waters."

I laid there for a few minutes, trying to figure out what was going on. Finally, I decided to investigate. I picked up my watch, and it said 6:00 am. I quickly went to the window to see if it was storming, but it was quiet. Next, I thought, well, maybe one of our friends in the other room couldn't sleep and listened to some kind of sound machine. I opened the door to the living room, and it was silent, but inside the room, I could hear "the sound of many waters," and the bed was still vibrating.

I crawled back into the bed, noticing Dave was still asleep. I know that I lay there for a good 30-40 minutes before everything subsided, but it had only been 15 minutes when I checked my phone!

Later, as we were getting ready for the day, I told Dave the story. I discovered that he had also felt the bed shaking in the middle of the night and thought, "Why in the world is she turning on the massager in the middle of the night?" I marveled at the visitation from God and the open portal we experienced; even if Dave was half asleep, we still felt it.

The following day, there was a stir as news of the encounter spread through our group. We were all standing around the large kitchen island, nibbling on breakfast as Allessia shared the encounter. Excitement and expectancy merged into a joyous exhibition when, Zapppp! A spark of electricity arced from Allessia's back to the wall. Gasps flew as heaven's energy filled the room. It was as if God was highlighting the moment with a rather shocking kiss from heaven.

"Years later," Allessia writes, "I feel like this encounter has a significance that I am still unpacking, but I think the thing that was the most significant to me was the sound I heard in the middle of the night. I have never heard anything like it, and the only way I could describe it is what the bible describes as the "sound of many waters," which is HIS VOICE. I feel like this was a throne room encounter. Time was of no consequence here, and the place I was in this moment vibrated and shook because the King was near. I know I was in a Holy moment."

All the weekend's encounters tied together, connecting the moves of God past and present, not only on the property but in the city. I believe this is a prophetic picture of God's desire for whole cities to become places where His presence is known.

Heaven is open. We have unhindered access as His sons and daughters. But some places seem to be direct downspouts where all feel his tangible presence. My heart is for everyone to realize that Heaven isn't shut. We can experience all that Jesus has for us. These heavenly portals always point back to the One who Himself is the Door, the Gateway, and the Portal—Jesus of Nazareth.

Activation

1. Portals can be the amazing stories shared in this chapter. They can also be the simple feeling of God's presence surrounding you. Ask Him to cover you now and wrap you in His arms.
2. Seeing in the Spirit is as easy as looking. Ask God to show you what His overshadowing presence looks like in the Spirit. You may see just a glimmer but keep looking and you'll both learn to

see more, and He will show you more along the
way.

3. Grow your gift! Keep looking, listening, and
   investigating all that God is doing in your life.
   Also, watch and listen to resources that will stir
   your spirit and ignite your faith. If you hear of God
   moving at a church or conference, GO! Taste and
   See what God is doing with different people in
   different places. Don't let a minor difference in
   belief prevent you from experiencing a move of
   God in another stream. God moves through those
   who are hungry and humble, not the ones who
   know so much that they refuse to go and sit at
   another's table. Be open, and remember, He will
   guard and protect your heart in all truth.

CHAPTER 8 | JESUS VISIONS

As He looked up, I realized it was Jesus. His eyes pierced my soul with eternity. They were earthy, rich brown, and natural. Yet another, deeper layer looked like electric blue lighting, full of the cosmos. Even in seeing Him on earth, He still had the countenance of when I saw Him in heaven, larger than the universe, with all creation reflecting as a twinkle in His eye.

Time and eternity fade when you lock eyes with Him.

Your mind remembers it.

Your body feels it.

Your soul reverberates it.

Your spirit expands it.

He lives in you. Yes, He was always there, even before you knew Him. But, even still, the first layer is becoming aware of His living love already surrounding you. Then you yield, giving your life to Him. This awakens you to Him, unlocking your access to everything He has already freely given you. But it's too much. It'll take time and eternity just to apprehend one ounce of His love for you.

The next layer is seeing who you are in Him. This removes the lies of everything you thought you weren't and reveals the truth of who you really are—His son, His daughter. Now you've discovered your identity, where you have faith, boldness, and courage to rise into who He has called you to be.

Layer after layer, He reveals more of Himself to you, revealing more of who you are to Him. In humility, you grow higher than you ever dream while being rooted in the grace and kindness that saved you and gave you new life. He equips you to soar into the heavenlies and make your discoveries known to the earth in the uniquely creative way that he made you. You have found your purpose, way, truth, and life in Him.

But there is more.

Jesus is the Aleph and Tav, Alpha and Omega, Beginning and End. All-encompassing, all-consuming fire—the lifeforce that burns within you, driving you passionately, deeply, and hopelessly lovesick into never-ending recesses of His heart.

As He takes you, you are His, and He is yours.

The more you eat of Him, the hungrier you become. Not because you lack, but because you've tasted and seen each bite gets better and better. He is the soothing of your soul and the quench of your thirst. With Him, you have everything. Without Him, you have nothing. He is your only want, need, and desire.

I have the same feeling after every encounter. I can't help but long for more of Jesus, whether it's amazing signs and wonders or a rendezvous with Jesus Himself. They are equally of His design because they come from Him and lead back to Him.

I don't take this lightly. I wish every day was an encounter with Jesus. Yes, metaphorically, mystically, or even naturally speaking, they are. But in this chapter. I want to share about a couple of actual encounters with Jesus Himself.

My Lament, My Rejoice

O' how is it that I can even write these words, my Lord? I am undone to share that I've actually seen you, believe it myself, and know it deeply.

Wretched man that I am, a sinner drowned in iniquity, deserving of death![55]

You exchanged Yourself for me, carried out my dept, and traded my death for your life![56]

Now, I am free. I have risen with you. Death could not overcome you. Now death has died, and life reigns with you![57]

Wretched without Him, at home within Him. I could now never call myself wretched again.[58] He

---

55 Romans 7:24
56 Galatians 2:20
57 Acts 2:31
58 Romans 8:1-3

cleansed me from that title and called me His own.[59]

Without Him, I am deceived by whom I am not—poor, blind, naked. With Him, I discover who I am—rich, seeing, clothed.[60]

Now I am found, no longer alone.[61] His name is in me, and the life I live, I live in Him.[62]

Encounters with Jesus Himself. How can I even attempt to write such things? It looms within me. Can I capture it in sincerity? Can I say to you in words what I experienced with Him?

A marvel—the tasks of Matthew, Mark, Luke, and John—much more than me, the power of their pen would mark eternity. How they must have felt, yet how could they resist? And how can I? They added to Scripture and I, a simple book. But His story must be told, and this is my story to tell.

The few lines above came out of nowhere. I had no idea what was about to happen. Yet, as the reality of what I was about to write pressed upon me in the opening section, a sobering wave of the Holy Spirit surrounded me. I will try to continue as best as I can in the fear of the Lord and the upmost respect for the subject matter. I know that my words will fall short, yet "when I am weak, He is strong." I pray you experience your own encounter with Jesus Himself as you read mine.

---

[59] 1 John 3:1, Hebrews 11:16
[60] Revelation 3:17-18
[61] Hebrews 13:5
[62] Galatians 4:19, Colossians 1:27

I don't know how many times I've seen Jesus in the ways I am about to share with you in a dream or vision. It is so seared in my mind that I envision it every time I think about it. And the more I look internally; the more His pulls me in like a tractor beam. His love causes me almost to live dual lives—one in Him, one in this world.

It's easy to recite that in retrospect, but in the moment, we can often be unaware[63] that we are even having an encounter, much less one with the King. Seeing Him, whether in human form or glory form, revelation from the Holy Spirit is needed to apprehend what's happening to us.

Aslan

I am sure that in eternity, we will see that we had many more encounters, dare I say face-to-face moments with Jesus than we could possibly imagine. It reminds me of the story of Shasta from CS Lewis' *The Horse and His Boy*. After meeting Aslan—a large lion who represents Jesus in the land of Narnia—for the first time, Aslan reveals that He has been there all His life, not just figuratively, but they had met several times without Shasta knowing who He really was.

"Who are you?" he said, barely above a whisper.

"One who has waited long for you to speak," said the Thing. Its voice was not loud, but very large and deep.

---

[63] Hebrews 13:2

Shasta thought he was alone when a stranger suddenly joined him on his journey through the night. He had heard of Aslan, but he wasn't told truths about Him.

Unaware that The Creator of Narnia accompanied him, Shasta feels frightened yet "reassured" by Him. Next, Shasta proceeds to tell the Stranger of all his adventures thus far in the story: his childhood, being chased by lions, dangers, hiding behind tombs from beasts, a journey through the desert, and another escape from a lion.

"Don't you think it was bad luck to meet so many lions?" said Shasta.

"There was only one lion." said the Voice.

"What on earth do you mean? I've just told you there were at least two lions the first night."

"There was only one, but he was swift of foot."

"How do you know?"

"I was the lion."

Aslan reveals that it was He who chased him early in the story so he would meet the companions to help him complete his journey. It was He who protected him from beasts at the tombs. And it was He who chased him once again to help them flee fast enough to escape a pursuing army.

If that wasn't enough, Aslan then reveals that He has also been with Shasta his whole life, and even pushed the boat he was in as a baby to ensure it reached the shore where a fisherman would take him in.

"Who are you?" asked Shasta.[64]

Aslan answered with a stoic, "Myself."

Shasta knew.

There was only One Lion, after all.

He had met Aslan.

When I read this, I was almost in tears. His view of his life was without God. In God's view of His life, He had always been there. Then, when He came near, God (Aslan) silently waited for Him to ask, and that was all Aslan needed to ignite their relationship.

Jesus Answers

As I read the bible this morning, I got stuck on one strikingly similar yet straightforward phrase, "Jesus answered." I shut my bible. I couldn't read more, "Jesus answered," kept running through my mind. Something I read a thousand times now rang like a bell inside my head, "Jesus answered."

In Shasta's life, Aslan was there even when he didn't know it. Before He even knew how to pray, Aslan (Jesus) answered. When he knew how to pray (talk to God), Aslan (Jesus) answered. It may not have been the answer that He wanted or expected, and that's not the point.

"Jesus answered."

Encounters are eye-openers, which is why testimonies are so powerful. They unlock the hardest of hearts because our stories create personal connections.

---

[64] C.S. Lewis, *The Horse and His Boy* (New York: Collier, 1954), p. 163-165.

I've seen the walls come down in the lives of people I ministered to over the years much faster through sharing the story of my relationship with God than debating about Him. Both have their place, but wise is the one who lets love guide.

When you can say to someone, "Jesus answered." It brings Him into their everyday lives through your story. "The man with experience is never at the mercy of a man with an argument," so the great quote tells us. The bible is a compilation of stories from those who've experienced God for this very reason. Therefore, we must be a people who experience God: A people who can say, "Jesus answers!"

We don't say, "Has God said?" a question born in the heart of the accuser's rebellion. Instead, we follow the voice of Jesus, "God has said," or "it is written."[65] It's a proclamation that Jesus is alive and active within us. His answers surround us, seeding doubt-bashing faith into those who receive our testimony.

Shasta now knows that Aslan is real, that He answers, and that He loved Him even before Shasta knew that He existed. In this passage alone, we could spend days digesting the brilliance of Lewis and the Christian life. I imagine that you've already been poked by Holy Spirit into remembering places you thought you were alone, but Jesus was there. Recognizing this is the first step. But what I love about this story is that Shasta had an actual encounter with Aslan (Jesus).

---

[65] Matthew 4:4-6

The Stranger

A "Beautiful Stranger" has often been a description of choice for those who have encounters with Jesus and only realize it either at the very last or in afterward. Sometimes, we question whether or not it was really Him or if He was really there. Shasta did this too, but when he looked down, he saw a large paw print in the ground that became a stream of refreshing water. So likewise, any (genuine) encounter with Jesus will have His fingerprints (pawprints) on it and become a stream of refreshing water. The effects will last. In fact, you won't be able to get away from them. After any encounter with Jesus, you'll be forever changed.

The Stranger idea emanates from the story of the Disciples on the road to Emmaus (Luke 24). No doubt that this is inspired Lewis. The chapter from the excerpt is even called "The Unwelcome Fellow Traveler." Just as cold drinks ship in six-packs, for now, we will only be able to open one bottle as I'll save the rest for a future conversation. There is so much here, so much Jesus is revealing about Himself, His nature, His love for His friends, and His eternal plan. But it was His hiddenness that intrigued me.

Jesus answers their questions, and they don't even realize it's Him. All they needed was right beside them, yet they were (somewhat) oblivious as their hearts gave way to the presence of the King and began to burn within them.

They knew Natural Jesus, they knew Teacher Jesus, they knew Miracle Jesus, they knew Agony Jesus, and they knew Crucifixion Jesus, but they had yet to meet

Resurrection Jesus. When He shows up, their eyes must be transformed to see Him. He was there the whole time, but they needed another touch from Him to lift their vision to where He was in the "today" of their lives.

The Stranger became a Friend when they recognized their friend as their resurrected Lord. Jesus — "Aslan was on the move." Jesus is always on the move. If we lose sight of His presence, we can always return to the last thing He said as a starting point for what He's presently doing in our lives. Holy Spirit keeps His words close to us, reminding us of His voice.[66]

Jesus laid a trail of "breadcrumbs" for the disciples to follow as He readied them for His transition from earth back to heaven.[67]

- Before Jesus died, He prepared them to see Him in His resurrection.
- Before His ascension, He prepared them to see Him Fly away.
- Now He reigns on high and has prepared them to recognize Him when He comes again, in the same way that He left.[68]

Jesus is always at rest, yet always on the move, always coming, always answering, always calling us higher, and always there. If we see Him in Stranger form, its because He is about to upgrade our view of Him. He is always guiding us from glory to glory.

---

[66] John 14:26
[67] John 6:35
[68] Mark 9:30-32, Acts 1-2

Cosmic Jesus

My story is kind of a reverse tale, as you read in the opening paragraph of this chapter. I have this reoccurring encounter where I see Jesus in the cosmos and the cosmos in Jesus. I see it almost daily but there have been a handful of actual encounters with Jesus in the same heavenly place.

Many will see Jesus in the natural setting or as a man before seeing Him in a heavenly setting as God. He is both, of course—the Hypostatic Union, but He uses both to speak to us in different ways. I am a macro thinker, so I go way out (as you've read) into the far reaches of the universe or heavenly places, then I come rapidly back down to earth for a natural reset. Thankfully, Jesus has shown Himself to me in both ways.

Seeing Him in opposite order (not that there is one) was key to me seeing just how amazing He was in the natural place. I gravitate towards the heavenly encounters but often find the parabolic side of Jesus more captivating as I climb into my mid-forties.

I can't recall the first moment of this encounter. It started off as what I thought was a trip to heaven or that I was seeing a vision of outer space. I also can't recall not having it for the last decade, so it must have begun in the early 2010s. I am not quite sure how I got there, but I do believe it was the precursor for the experience in chapter four. My heart was hungry for third heaven encounters when I embarked on this interstellar expedition.

There is an activation I do that inspires the imagination to see the universe in God's perspective. I have people close their eyes and picture themselves flying across the cosmos like one of those YouTube videos[69] that zooms out the give the human mind a reference point for the scale of space. I'll take you through it in the activation for this chapter. Getting God's eye view causes us to see Him differently than we would in a natural setting. Picturing Him this way transforms our mental scale of His majesty and expands our perception of reality.

If we see Him in a video that seeks to show the scale of the universe, He will reveal Himself to us in that way. Life experiences come together in moments of elevation when He suddenly shows up, walks beside us, and takes us into a new dimension—an Emmaus encounter.

For me, it all came together in a vision. It started when I saw what looked like earth. I knew I was hovering somewhere in space. I didn't feel like I was in our solar system, though. It felt like I was way, way out there. Trying to write almost shuts down my brain because when I think about the celestial landscapes around me in this heavenly place, the scope is beyond comprehension. However, my initial view was small compared to what was to come. The planet was blue and beautiful, then it was done.

Space is very captivating to me, which is why God probably showed it to me to begin with, as you've already read throughout this book. Holding it close to my heart, I found I was there again and again. I'm not sure if it was a dreamlike state, vision, or trance. This time, I was

---

[69] The Observable Universe:
https://youtu.be/HiN6Ag5-DrU (scan qr code)

further away and got a better view of my peripheral surroundings.

Where am I?

Am I seeing earth from a different dimension?

The enormity of what was going on in the background was indescribable. There was light, a Presence, plants, stars, galaxies, nebula and other objects I've never seen before.

In the next vision, I was right back in the same place. Looking at myself looking at a planet, which this time appeared to be Saturn, just as you would see it in one of those new HD pictures, only this was at least five years before they were published.

Trips to this heavenly place became common for a season lasting over two years. I would find myself here in prayer as it kinda became my secret place with the Lord. Each time I would see a little more detail. I saw more planets and more spacey things going on as if building toward something. I thought I was honing my spiritual sight and perception, which I was, but there was much more, both near and far, with varying degrees of detail.

I would always try to zoom in to see more detail and ascertain why I was there and what was going on. Finally, I was able to move a little closer, but I would reach a certain point, and that was it. I speculated why I couldn't go further, not that there was a problem, but maybe I was missing something.

Then I had a subtle inkling to look up, seeing some other planets and cosmic objects. I realized that none of it was random. Instead, they intertwined into a cosmic gear system. The planets had the same blue hue as earth yet were energized with a vibrant glow. Each was like a brushstroke of a larger picture.

Suddenly, I went flying backward some distance, but I didn't feel like I had moved at all in such an expansive space. From further away, I saw that the clusters of planets and stars formed an iris.

Hairs rose on my arm as emotions of bliss, fear, and joy ran my mind through a state of disbelief. My thoughts assembled like the picture before me, forming an image in my mind of whose iris it was that my eyes were beholding.

Jesus.

I couldn't see the rest of His face yet, not even His eye. It was only the round of the iris, like an apparition in space.

"Who else could it be?"

The power.

The majesty.

The Holy Spirit, alive in me as the radar of truth, pinging on the power source of time and eternity, told me who. I saw the entirety of the cosmos in His eyes. I had to fight intensely to stay in the encounter, just like I am fighting to write about it now.

Over the subsequent encounters, I both soared and struggled. I wanted to go further out and see Jesus' face, but it was overwhelming. It lasted another whole season.

I would see the earth, then zoom out and see His eye, then try to go further and see His face. Each time, part of me changed. With each glimpse, my capacity to see more increased.

Eventually, step by celestial step, I made it—I saw the face of Jesus in the cosmos. Like the eye, His entire face was made up of all creation. I saw layer upon layer of unknown shapes and indescribable objects. I saw how He holds the stars in His hands and how small the universe(s) is in His presence.[70] His majesty is beyond measure.

I didn't just see planets. I saw their lifecycles firing at His will, harmonizing with the song of life embedded in its programming. Rebirth, expansion, and life. Flash, upward spirals, and procreation. Life-giving and endless joy is in the One who created all and holds all things together.

Human Jesus

While this Jesus vision doesn't even begin to encapsulate Him, I did see Him in a much more expanded state than ever before. How did this Being, this Entity—God Himself, the Eternal Son, step foot on the earth? The universe itself cannot contain Him. Seeing Him in this state, there would be no question that Jesus is Lord, the Most High, and King of Everything.[71] We would certainly bow in awe, but would we know Him intimately—a God who is like His own creation? Probably not. It's too big a vision, too vast for human comprehension. Jesus wants

---

[70] Revelation 1:16
[71] Revelation 19:16

us to know Him in all the ways He's made Himself available to be known. His life on earth was the onramp for His majesty and the doorway for us to see Him in ever-increasing glory. He created us for this. He went from His cosmic form to the form of a man so that we would have that connection point. Holy Spirit activates our spirits to see and perceive what our minds cannot—Jesus full of glory. Let's revisit Paul's explanation:

> He existed in the form of God, yet he gave no thought to seizing equality with God as his supreme prize. Instead he emptied himself of his outward glory by reducing himself to the form of a lowly servant. He became human! He humbled himself and became vulnerable, choosing to be revealed as a man and was obedient. He was a perfect example, even in his death—a criminal's death by crucifixion! Because of that obedience, God exalted him and multiplied his greatness! He has now been given the greatest of all names! The authority of the name of Jesus causes every knee to bow in reverence! Everything and everyone will one day submit to this name—in the heavenly realm, in the earthly realm, and in the demonic realm. And every tongue will proclaim in every language: "Jesus Christ is Lord Yahweh," bringing glory and honor to God, his Father!

> Philippians 2:6-11 TPT

The story of Jesus in the Gospels is our connection point to His earthly life and access point to His heavenly glory. In reading them and getting to know my Savior, I was given a vision of Jesus Himself being the One who is the Source and Life of all things. This grandeur expands when we realize that the heavenlies were contained within Him when He was on the earth. He was both overseeing the universe and living within it at the same time.

> No one has ascended to heaven but He who came down from heaven, that is, the Son of Man who is in heaven.
>
> John 3:13 KJV

In seeing our Creator like this, we see that in His image, we are also on earth but coexist in heavenly places:

> But God, being rich in mercy, because of the great love with which he loved us, even when we were dead in our trespasses, made us alive together with Christ—by grace you have been saved—and **raised us up with him** and **seated us with him in the heavenly places** in Christ Jesus, so that in the coming ages he might show the immeasurable riches of his grace in kindness toward us in Christ Jesus.
>
> Ephesians 2:4-7 ESV *emphasis mine*

The one who reigns above all became one of us to transition us from our lowest place and seat us with Him in His highest place. His ascension was our ascension. He brought us up to rule and reign with Him as kingdom family. Experiencing Jesus in heavenly or cosmic places is as natural as seeing Him in those around us. He made us like Him by restoring us to the image of His Father made of us before the fall, which was in the image of Jesus before the creation.

As cosmic as Jesus was in the last encounter, He is also all of us.

> And the King will answer them, 'Truly, I say to you, as you did it to one of the least of these my brothers, you did it to me.'

> Matthew 25:40 ESV

Jesus used the phrase, "Son of Man," about Himself more than any other. Just as I saw the galaxies in Him, all of humanity also exists in Him. And He, according to this verse, exists in them. We miss Jesus if we fail to love our neighbor. Paul clarifies this in the Love Chapter.[72] If I see His heavenly glory but miss His earthly heart, then I miss the point of the revelation. Seeing Him down to earth in daily life is just as necessary and marvelous as the heavenly encounters if we have eyes to see.

The Man I didn't know I knew

The date in my journal says March 17th, 2018. As I write this, it's March 11th, 2022. Nearly four years to the day of recording the encounter I am about to share with you. It is one of those on heaven on earth moments that reveals the humanity of Jesus:

Not too long ago, as I was lying in my bed somewhere between asleep and awake, I was taken into a vision. I was walking in an otherworldly plane that felt like somewhere between heaven and earth, although I could

---

[72] Read 1 Corinthians 13 for context.

feel the hard, cracked ground beneath my feet. It was hard to distinguish between earth and sky. A beige color saturated my environment in a desert-like setting.

Instantly, a man walks past me. His white robe shimmered and flowed with a golden hem on His garment. My eyes raced towards His outline as He was nearly gone. He turned His head just enough for me to realize it was Jesus. In the next moment, He was out of frame.

Gone.

I ran after Him.

I entered a new frame, just as He was already leaving (like going from scene to scene in a movie). The setting was the same but there were people around. However, they were very vague and distant.

"It's Jesus! It's Jesus!"

No response.

I tried to keep up with Him and moved quickly to the next frame. But, again, He walked out just as I walked in and seemed a little further away.

The people in this frame were more visible.

"It's Jesus! It's Jesus!"

I became frustrated as they likewise didn't seem to respond or even acknowledge Jesus in their proximity.

I followed Him into the fourth frame.

This time, it was only Him. He walked from my left to right and out of frame again. As He did, the background disappeared behind him for a moment. Once He had passed me, I looked to see a stranger sitting on a curb right in front of me. I stopped for a moment and observed my surroundings. No one else was nearby. The environment had not changed, still a misty tan with earth and sky both the same color.

I looked down at the stranger, intent on telling him that Jesus had just passed by him. The curb he sat on had faded red paint like that of a fire lane. He sat in a squat position and wore a robe, not unlike Jesus', but the color seemed to match the environment. His head was down, covered by a hood.

I went up to him and said, "Jesus just walked right in front of you."

Slowly, he raised his head. And to my surprise, his peripheral matched that of Jesus from the first scene.

A thought flashed through my head.

"What if this IS Jesus?"

"What if He looks at me? What do I do?"

His head continued to turn until He locked eyes with me. His complexion was dark, like a deep tan. His hair was dark brown with a beard to match.

He pulled back His hood, and I was absorbed into an encounter with His face. His eyes were a hazel brown like I'd never seen them before. The irises began to move and reveal multi-layers of dimension as if they were reacting to my heart's level of receptivity. His singular look into my eyes was like a hundred. It felt like jolts of energy passing through both my body and soul. My senses were on rapid-fire, trying to collect and record the face of infinity. The magnitude of His stare phased through me, pulsating in my being. Shockwaves of power emanated from His eyes. With each one, the atmosphere, color, sound, light, and sound changed. The pulsations felt like they contained the universe. A singular glance into His eyes revealed the enormity of the cosmos.

At the same time, it was the most down-to-earth and personal I had ever seen Him. The way He looked at me is why there is a word called love.

He knew me.

He came to me.

His walk in the first three scenes was to draw me to Himself. This vision was my Road to Emmaus experience. I followed the heavenly Jesus, who introduced me to the human Jesus, so I could get to know Him better both in heaven and on earth. Just as the disciples had known Him in an array of ways, I was now learning to know Him in a new way.

The Stranger was my Friend. He set a trap for me with Himself and lured me into Him, "hook, line, and sinker." I took the bait. I felt seen, known, and heard.

The waves of love continued until I sat upright in my bed. I had seen Him before, but now I have a glimpse into what it may have been like to see Him in His earthly life. I will never forget how He looked up at me as if One who was lovesick no longer. I am forever changed!

If this encounter was a vision, how many times was He right there in front of me in real life, and I didn't know it? Yes, I want to see Him in majesty, but I don't want to miss Him in humanity. I saw the same eyes in both His cosmic form and His human form. Even as a man, He is still King of Kings.

Shasta had encountered Aslan many times before He knew Him. That's okay; that's how Jesus woo's our hearts. Shasta had a turning point. From then on, He knew Him whom He did not know. My prayer is that you will know Him in heaven and on earth. That center of your life will hone in on His love for you.

Activation

1. Draw a dot in the center of your hand. Now, imagine you are looking down at yourself from above. Like you're in a hot air balloon, you rise above your house, neighborhood, city, and state. Now you can see your whole country, the oceans, and the earth. Next, you accelerate past the moon, the solar system, and the galaxy. Faster than the speed of light, passing clusters of galaxies along the way. Further you go as they come together, billions at a time. You see the entire expanse of the universe. Now, look at the dot in your hand. That dot is the universe in the hand of God. God doesn't live somewhere in the universe; He is a higher realm in Himself. Now that you've seen Him this way, you can experience Him on a whole new level. Now, you see why David thought

Goliath was so small. When you use God as He is, you'll know there is nothing He can't do.[73]

2. Place yourself in the second Jesus vision. Imagine that you see Him just as I did—as a simple man, sitting on a curb. Slowly, He looks up and locks eyes with you. Infinite love and power flow through you. Once you see Jesus like this, you receive and give love like we never have before.

---

[73] Video of activation featuring David Edwards, Leif Hetland, and Scott Thompson: https://youtu.be/pi7fxaCuTPw (scan qr code)

CHAPTER 9 | TIME DILATION

An emerald flash encircles the earth. A beam of light shines skyward, stretching beyond the heavens.

Earth reborn.

A mystery revealed.

A time at end.

Timelessness begins.

In the end as in the beginning.

All things restored—all things new.

"Wait, did I just travel through time?"

Ends Are Beginnings

Where is this all going? What is the outcome, end day, grand finale? There are many opinions, doctrines, and beliefs about what the end will look like. Theologians call the study and consideration of such things, "eschatology." It means the study of the "last things" or days. Many believe that we are on the verge of the second coming of Jesus. How this occurs is usually subdivided into a plethora of belief systems. There are many studies available that explain what these theories are. It's often a touchy topic to consider as many have strong convictions that their doctrine is true and all others are not only false but "end-times deceptions." I often joke that no one knows precisely how it will unfold because "it hasn't happened yet." But even in that, some would suggest that it has.

I don't want to dive into all of it here, rather, I will continue to tell you the stories of amazing heavenly encounters. However, I will give you a grid for my belief system, which can be summarized in family and revival. To see what happens in the end, we must look at the beginning. When we do, we see a Family:

A Father loving His Son.

The Son loving the Spirit.

The Spirit loving the Father.

No matter which direction the love flows, you see the Family of the Trinity emanating their desire to create, redeem, and enjoy a loving relationship with their sons and daughters.

The Father's heart for family sets the pattern for creation. If you read from Genesis to Jesus, then from Jesus to Revelation, in light of the family blueprint, it will transform how you read the bible and view eschatology. Without this story arc, we will miss the Creator's heart and intention for creation.

The Father commissions His earthly family—His son Adam, and His daughter, Eve—to cover the earth with this family expression.

> And God blessed them. And God said to them, "Be fruitful and multiply and fill the earth and subdue it, and **have dominion** over the fish of the sea and over the birds of the heavens and over every living thing that moves on the earth."
>
> Genesis 1:28 ESV *emphasis mine*

We know that they sadly failed to complete this commission. Therefore, the Father, in His infinite wisdom, would demonstrate His ultimate act of love by sending His son, Jesus, to restore His family to the Creator's image, empowering them to follow His example and continue the commission.

> And proclaim as you go, saying "the **kingdom of heaven** is at hand. Heal the sick, raise the dead, cleanse the lepers, cast out demons.
>
> And Jesus came and said to them, "All authority in heaven and on earth has been given to me. Go therefore and make disciples of all nations, baptizing them in the name of the Father and of the Son and of the Holy Spirit, teaching them to observe all that I have commanded you. And behold, **I am with you always**, to the end of the age."
>
> Matt 10:7-8, 28:18-20 ESV *emphasis mine*

The disciples were commanded to take the kingdom, "King's Dominion," to all nations, making them disciples who would discover their place in the kingdom family. We see the original commission in Genesis, and the recommission by Jesus for the family expression in the garden to cover the cosmos—restoring to the Father's original design.

Jesus not only sends them out as family ambassadors but says that He will be with them *always*. As the family expands (preaching the gospel and transforming nations), the light will shine across the earth. The "end of the age" is congruent with Him *always* being with us. What He started in His life continued through His disciples in Acts and flows throughout church history to us today. I believe that revival will spread like wildfire across the planet and culminate in what the bible calls the Great Wedding Feast at the end of the age (Mt 22, Rev 19). It begins with family and culminates in a family celebration—forming a cycle from the creation of family to the union of Creator and creation.

You may view it differently, and that's alright with me. However, I hope that this extends your consideration of it.

From this angle, we can begin to answer some of the questions presented: Where is it all going? To where it all began. Not a repeat, but a rebirth. The family is born again or born from above—*anothen*—in His image. And, as the cycle completes, the heavens and the earth will be born again—born from above!

All creation groans for this and we groan too that all things and all people will come to accept the invitation into the family. The bible says that some will not. They will choose to remain outside of His family, even after He has done everything to restore them to where He created them to be forever. Everyone will be judged accordingly, and those who refuse the invitation[74] will enter eternity without Him. I pray these words pierce your heart as His love is waiting for your "yes." Existence without Him is hell, both here and in the hereafter. But existence with Him is bliss, both here and the hereafter. Even in trial, we rejoice because we know we are part of the family. At the end of this chapter, I will lead you in prayer if your heart burns within you to know your place in the family is secure.

The bible says that as this age concludes, a new one emerges:

Then I saw a new heaven and a new earth, for the first heaven and the first earth had passed away, and the sea was no more. And I saw the holy city, new Jerusalem, coming down out of heaven from God, prepared as a bride adorned for her husband. And I heard a loud voice from the throne saying, "Behold, the dwelling place of God is with man. He will dwell with them, and they will be his people, and God himself will be with them as their God. He will wipe away every tear from their eyes, and death shall be no more, neither shall there be mourning, nor crying, nor pain anymore, for the former things have passed away." And he who was seated on the throne said, "Behold, I am making all things new." Also he said, "Write this down, for these words are trustworthy and true." And he said to me, "It is

---

[74] Read Matthew 22 for context.

done! I am the Alpha and the Omega, the beginning and the end.

Revelation 21:1-5a ESV

Family is complete. The spiral from beginning to end has reached a new beginning. The Apostle Peter says a flash of fire will accompany this rebirth, removing all that existed outside of His image, (I'll expand on this momentarily). The heavens and earth baptized in fire making a new dwelling for His family, just as He made one in the beginning.

Formed in Goodness

Adam was the imager of God. He was created on the seventh day because the Father prepared a space for Him to dwell. If we look at the six days of creation that precede this, we see God forming and filling spaces for creation.

In his book, *How Not to Read the Bible,* Dan Kimball explains the Hebraic perspective of the story of creation found in Genesis. We often read it chronologically. However, the storyteller would view time as a spiraling expansion. Each day is like a lens stacked on the previous day through which we can look down and see both the macro and micro perspectives. Genesis and Revelation have a similar structure as they sound somewhat repetitive from a Western point of view, but from the contextual angle, they present a macro view followed by micro details. Considering this, let's look at Kimball's exposition of the literary context in Genesis one:

A surface level reading of Genesis 1 and the six days often misses the literary-artistic design of the Hebrew text. A closer look reveals a parallel structure in which the first three days of creation parallel the last three days. We catch hints of this framework in Genesis 1:2 when it states, "The earth was formless and empty." This sets up our expectations for what comes next. God is about to take what was formless and, in the first three days, will give it form and function. After He forms it, He fills it. Days 1—3 deal with the formlessness of the earth, giving it shape and function. Days 4—6 deal with the void, filling what was empty.[75]

He then goes on to illustrate each of the six days and how the sequence of forming and fulling progress in this chart:

Forming	Filling
Day 1: light and darkness	Day 4: the lights of day and night
Day 2: sky and sea	Day 5: birds and fish
Day 3: fertile earth	Day 6: land animals, including man[76]

After each forming and filling, "God looked at all He had made and saw that it was good." Goodness was the container for the creation of sons and daughters in His

---

[75] Dan Kimball, *How Not to Read the Bible* (Grand Rapid: Zondervan, 2020), p. 191.
[76] Ibid.

image. Goodness would be their dwelling. After He created man, His statement about His creation elevates from "good" to "very good."[77] This is the goodness they, as His family, were to fill the rest of creation with. As we saw earlier, this was restored in Jesus—the Second Adam—showing us our call as family to reproduce and cover the earth with His goodness. Goodness dwells in light. As the light shines, the containers of darkness shatter and His glory burns brighter until the culmination of the age. In the end, His statement will match the announcement made at the beginning, "It is good."

We see Him say it about Jesus, first at His water baptism and second at His transfiguration. This shows that His desire is for both natural (water) and supernatural (light) to be immersed and transformed in His goodness. God is good, which is revealed through the love of His family who demonstrate the power and wisdom of the Spirit to all creation, returning them to their place in His design.

The creation of Adam was also implemented through forming and filling. The word "image" in Hebrew is *tselem,* which means outline, shadow, form, or imprint. Some say God molded man from clay, which may be true, but when we view Genesis 1:27 and 2:7 as layers to see the whole story, another angle emerges.[78]

Imagine lying down and making a snow angel. When you stand back up, the form of the angel is still there, right where your body was. It's not you, but it is your

---

77 Genesis 1:3-25; 31
78 Read both chapters in full for context.

form. What if, in the same way, God imprinted His form into the earth and then breathed life back into His form? It's not Him, but it is His image with His life animating the new creation. First, He formed it (imprint) and then filled it (breath). Adam was made of the very substance of God Himself. Jesus is God Himself, filling the form—stepping into the womb of creation and walking among us to fulfill God's image in the earth.

Another way to say it is that Adam was God's form yet fell outside of His image. Jesus put on Adam's form (Second Adam) and remained in the image. The original Adam became the tainted form. The New Adam (Jesus) is the untainted form. Jesus, the Untainted One, allowed all that was outside of His image (form) to be placed on Him, taking it to its death. He then rose to life, having cleansed the First Adam (humankind) from all sin (anything outside God's image) and restored (metanoia) the tainted form with the untainted form.[79]

Can you see the dance between Genesis and Revelation and how the life of Jesus ties them together? When His form (image) isn't present, we fill the void with Jesus (or He with us). As His family, we operate as His agency of transformation—church (ekklesia) in the earth.

Wherever there is a love deficit, He desires to fill it with His love. Wherever there is sickness, He desires to fill it with His healing. Wherever there is hopelessness, He desires to fill it with His hope. The Gospel is both the salvation (form) and the Spirit (filling) needed for His image to be seen, known, and heard in the earth. First,

---

[79] Revisit Hebrews 1:3-4 and Colossians 1:15-20, which articulate Jesus as the form of God, His "exact image," and how He "reconciled all things" to Himself (God's image).

the church was formed, then it was required to be filled before it could complete the commission of covering the earth with the King's dominion (Acts 1-2), reuniting the earth with His will in heavenly places.

I believe this is why encounters are important. As emissaries of the celestial, we must know what the celestial is like. We are welcome into heavenly places. The Lord's prayer is a prayer of ascension. "Your kingdom come," means that we must learn our identity in Him as sons and daughters who reign in life from our heavenly seat. This isn't just a metaphor; it's a reality.

Some heavenly encounters are kisses from heaven with various purposes. Others see to leave the earthly behind and step behind the veil where we are in the throne room or with the King in His heavenly dimension. Typically, these are apocalyptic in nature. I am not saying they are on par with apocalyptic literature in scripture; rather, the scripture is the anchor point and invitation for us to also encounter God in this way, stepping outside of the veil, even outside of time.

Outside of Time

How did I get there...to the end of time?

Well...I was at church...worshipping the Lord.

Then...Woosh!

It took a while to drive from the south side of metro Atlanta to the North as we navigated through rush hour. Flustered, but not too much, we found some seats and settled as the meeting began. Dear friend, Shay Arthur, invited us to make the urban trek to hear her share the word that evening. Other friends, Hayley and Heidi (who you met in chapter one), were ready to lead us into worship. I like to see the room and move around during the set. I want to see what the Lord is doing in both realms. The back usually gives me the best vantage point. So, I found a place along the wall and turned my inner gaze towards His face. I became aware of His presence, which was already permeating the room as many were ascending to the throne. I smiled as I knew these strangers were friends in the spirit and knew the Lord.

No time seemed to pass before the room got a little fuzzy. It wasn't due to less vision but greater. I began to see details that were normally missed, coupled with heightened spiritual activity. The natural and supernatural were layered together. I see in the spirit like this often, but I wasn't ready for what was about to happen.

Zoom!

The room accelerated, pulling me out of time. It reminded me of a movie came out a few years ago about unlocking the full potential of the human brain. The climax contained a scene showing the protagonist going back in time as if it was all rewinding. Ages and civilizations went from empires to wildernesses as she fast-reversed to the beginning of human evolution. While I am not a proponent of macro-evolution, the scene gives an illustrative glimpse into God's limitless power towards those who believe.[80]

---

[80] Read Ephesians 1:15-23 for context: Advances in technology (CGI in movies) can show us ways to ponder all possibilities in God. While if used for evil, it has its vices. But, if used from God's intention, it can heighten humanity and inspire our spiritual life in ways never

Yet, in my encounter, I was going forward in time. All the people in the room sped up around me, going about the service, leaving, night falling, sun rising, day in and out—all in less than a millisecond. Time accelerated into a blur—sun rising, setting, rising again, people being born, living, dying, rising. Generations were like lightning strikes, making an amazing flash but giving away to the next as their light was catalogued in the annals of history.

I saw buildings and cities rise and fall and transform. Landscapes also changed as mountains stood up out of valleys and stooped back down again. The greens of the field yielded to houses and roads as places that were houses and roads became green again.

The circle of life spun faster and faster, yet brighter and brighter. Each generation was closer to the image of God as His kingdom spread across the earth.

Was it a hundred generations? Was it a thousand? I am unsure, and I don't think chronology was the point. The faster you go, the more everything slows down because you begin to see everything at once. Physics calls this "time dilation." If you go fast enough, you become light. Your point of reference sees the timeline as a whole. You step outside of it and see it from God's perspective. You see the texture, color, and reality of time. Past, present, and future are all seen simultaneously from the same vantage point.

As I sped up, I slowed down.

---

seen before. In this passage, Paul explains how the Holy Spirit can unlock our full potential as human beings—another way of viewing metanoia.

Rest.

Jesus. Alpha. Omega. Beginning. End.

Begin Again.

He reigns above all, is in all, and sees all.

The testimony of Jesus is the spirit of prophecy[81] because all things flow through Him. He stepped into time as the timeless one. He allowed time to contain Him so He could find us in the timeline and reset us in His image both within the timeline and heavenly places. This perspective gives us eyes to see and ears to hear what the Spirit says—inside time and outside time. We prophesy from our vantage point outside of time, seeing the macro picture and how it affects our micro lives. In doing so, we see how big we really are in Him. The point isn't to prophesy chronology but His reality. The chronology changes because He is patient and wants everyone to come to know Him.[82] That's His heart's desire. As time flows, He's looking for those looking for Him through which He can transform creation with His love.

Even in the slowness, I felt as if time had dilated. I arrived at the end of time faster than I thought. All of the details, generations, and the changes I experienced along the way occurred in mere seconds—the encounter warped time as more things happened in those moments than the time allotted. Time seems to bend when heaven touches earth, as illustrated by Allessia's time-dilating watches.

---

[81] Revelation 19:10
[82] 2 Peter 3:8, which we will expound upon momentarily.

During the process of traveling through time, I slowly rose above the earth. I saw it spinning, year after year, decade after decade, and century after century. Then, it suddenly stopped. As I reached the end of time, time itself slowed down. Time's time had come.

What I am about to share isn't a dogmatic declaration of how the end of all things will occur. Not at all. Neither has this story been a timeline for eschatological events. Much of the theology I presented in this chapter was to cause us to think differently than that. This is simply something the Lord showed me in my own encounter that I am sharing with you to inspire you to experience Him.

When we train our students at School of Revivalists to prophesy, we follow protocols of kingdom culture to ensure that someone doesn't misapply a prophecy and derail their life because they thought the Lord was speaking direct events to them. Rather, we share what we feel the Lord is saying to inspire them to hear from God themselves. We avoid prophesying things like "dates, mates, babies, correction, and direction," which is wise advice we inherited from Bethel. That doesn't mean that God never speaks these things. However, we are careful not to be misheard or for the prophecy to be misunderstood. That is my goal here. It's simply a heavenly encounter—outside of time—that may become a motivation for others. It's not directional or emphatic, but a story, an experience, and an invitation for more.

New Heavens & New Earth

So, dear friends, don't let this one thing escape your notice: a single day counts like a thousand years to the Lord Yahweh, and a thousand years counts as one day. This means that, contrary to man's perspective, the Lord is not late with his promise to return, as some measure lateness. But rather, his "delay" simply reveals his loving patience toward you, because he does not want any to perish but all to come to repentance.

The day of the Lord will come and take everyone by surprise—as unexpected as a home invasion. The atmosphere will be set on fire and vanish with a horrific roar, and the heavenly bodies will melt away as in a tremendous blaze. The earth and every activity of man will be laid bare. Since all these things are on the verge of being dismantled, don't you see how vital it is to live a holy life? We must be consumed with godliness while we anticipate and help to speed up the coming of the day of God, when the atmosphere will be set on fire and the heavenly bodies consumed in a blaze. But as we wait, we trust in God's royal proclamation to be fulfilled. There are coming heavens new in quality, and an earth new in quality, where righteousness will be fully at home.

2 Peter 3:8-13 TPT

This passage encapsulates my experience. Whether a thousand years or day, Jesus is coming, and He's coming soon. We set our hearts to fulfill the great commission and accelerate His appearing when we live this way. Peter addressed this passage to those scoffing at the Gospel, just as they sneered at Noah for building an ark. And just as the earth was flooded with water in his day; it will be baptized in fire at the Day of the Lord. The fire will permanently remove all that remains outside of His family (form). Still, His heart continues to extend the grace of repentance so as many can come into the kingdom as will choose to.

Reality check: When I used to read this verse, the fear of the Lord would come upon me—as it should all of us. It calls us into account to live from who we are in Him, not from who we are not outside of Him. Verses like this are necessary for our lives to remain aligned with His. However, as John did earlier, Peter goes apocalyptic for a few moments, spiraling outside of time itself. The language here goes back to His Master speaking of new heavens and a new earth.

Heaven and earth will pass away, but my words
will not pass away.

Matthew 24:35 ESV

Heaven and earth both experienced rebellions. Heavenly beings—elohim—rebelled against God—Elohim. Mankind also rebelled, resulting in the fall. The realms of heaven and earth must now be baptized in fire and reborn in His image, as they were always intended. The news that both John and Peter talk about gives us the picture of heaven and earth being born again, experiencing metanoia and transfiguration. It's easy to view these passages only from the perspective of what the Lord is removing rather than from the outlook that He is transforming everything in the best possible way, giving new space and life where heaven and earth are one. This union was in Jesus, is in us now, and is coming. The nature of prophecy is that it has ever-expanding fulfillment. The picture we see formed in these verses in light of the pattern of Apocalyptic Literature shows us something beautiful. I believe this is the viewpoint the Lord gave in the encounter.

The Spark of Life

I was hovering above the earth like Superman when energized by the sun. The world shone with light, although it appeared to vignette on the edges of my frame of reference. An expanse rose above and behind it like a dimensional array of clouds, nebula, and light. There were stars around, and I was aware of other planets, the sun, and indescribable things mentioned in my Jesus vision.

The earth's rotation stilled.

Blazing emerald light flared as it encompassed the earth. Then, like a spotlight at a concert, a concentrated field of light shot from the surface into the heavens, brighter than the cosmos.

Rebirth.

There were blue and green hues of light mixed with white radiance. All was reborn in an instant, from molecules to stars. The earth was the same yet different—new, transformed.

It instantly reminded me of a video that captured the moment sperm fertilizes an egg. A flash occurs as two become one, and the spirit enters the new human. They referred to this as the "spark of life." I felt like I watched this happen on a celestial scale.

Spark—New Life.

New Heavens.

New Earth.

All One in Him.

The experience was exhilarating. I had traveled to the end of time, and it wasn't at all what I had expected. We often dial up images of death and destruction, but that wasn't the focus. Instead, the focus was on life: Life in newness, life in joy, and life in light. The fire was for purification, but it was also the spark of life. The spaces of heaven and earth were reborn, renewed, and reunited. His word became life as all remnants of "Has God said," released into creation by the fallen one were burned away. "It is good" ripples throughout the cosmos in the light of the Son.

From the end back to the now…

Worship was still going.

I was still leaning against the wall.

All returned to normal.

I am not sure how long I was gone, as two or three songs may have passed. I didn't know what to do for a few moments, so I just got down on my knees and worshiped Jesus.

It took a few moments to stabilize in the natural environment as I cherished the journey "there and back again."

In wonder, I gave thanks.

Activation

1. Eternity is wonderful, real, and blissful for those who know Jesus. If you feel like you weren't sure of your eternal condition as you read this chapter, pray this prayer with me:

   "Lord Jesus, I accept your invitation into the family. I receive your love and your life. You died for me so I could live forever with you. I choose right now to give you my heart. I turn away from all that is without you in word, action, and thought, knowing you will guide each step in your love, grace, and forgiveness. My life is yours, forever!"

2. It's a relationship. Your life is now His. Get connected to a kingdom minded family of believers to grow in your relationship with Him. Welcome home, welcome to the family of God!

CHAPTER 10 | THE EXPANSE

A new dimension broke through the sky. It appeared as a gradient of golden fire into translucent white light. This realm wasn't merely visiting ours; it was engulfing it. Eminent life and vitality invigorated the atmosphere. It energized the natural realm like a much-needed power source, infusing the substance of heaven into the earth.

Cloud prisms scattered majestic colors into dancing rainbows across the sky. Purity and power hummed in the center of the expanse. The brightest and whitest emanated from there, with impulses erupting from it like a fountain in all directions. The light gave life to all creation.

But it wasn't an object or some celestial body. It was alive. I was raptured as I looked, glancing ever so softly as love filled my gaze. I already knew that I would have to step outside of myself to engage the One who had come to engage me. I was in the presence of my King.

Heaven Opens

A book of ascent and a duology of encounters could not be complete without including one of the most significant encounters of my life. I wrote about it in my first book, *The Call for Revivalists*. In the following paragraphs, I'll add some extra details to the story and interweave them into the themes prevalent throughout *Mesmerize* as the dream gives an apocalyptic picture of the church through the ages. As I revisit this encounter, I am in awe that 21 years have passed since I had the dream, yet it only shines brighter with each look.

In the dream, I was sitting in a rock quarry. Its shape was like an amphitheater with a pool of water at the bottom. An open sky shined in the center, where the stage would have been. People assembled all around me like I was sitting in a stadium. I was in the middle of the rock face, next to a booth that looked like something out of the Flintstones. Inside the booth was Dr. Robert Gladstone, a teacher of mine from ministry school. Being prophetic, he represented the role of a prophet in the dream. He would phase or transfigure himself into Jesus and then back again—repeatedly. To his left was my friend Brandon, who also had a friend to his left. Likewise, I had a friend sitting to my right.

The rock quarry and the people gathered together in it represented the church. There was an atmosphere of expectation all around us. It was as if we were all waiting for something. I kept looking to the prophet sitting in the booth to gauge the spiritual climate and how I should respond to it.

Suddenly, to the right of the quarry, an enormous cloud drifted into frame. It had a dark-flat-blueish-gray tone. All at once, the feeling of fear arose within the church. I began to think about what clouds represent in Scripture. Immediately, my mind went to the glory cloud on Mt. Sinai and the glory filling King Solomon's temple. However, something didn't sit well with my spirit. It looked right, but it felt wrong. Many of the people began to freak out, shouting, "It is the Lord! Jesus is coming!" Their voices seemed to echo the feeling of fear that had accompanied the cloud.

Again, I looked to the prophet, who had maintained the figure of the teacher, no longer phasing into and out of Jesus. There was a sharp look of concern coupled with agitation on his face. He remained silent. His silence, however, spoke louder to me than the explosions of suspicious praise floating around the amphitheater. His look confirmed what I felt on the inside. I joined him in silence and our friends, who also followed his lead. Others took notice and accompanied our protest.

The event was quite chaotic. Different people responded in different ways, which coincided with where they were in life, their relationship with Jesus, and those in attendance.

Next, the cloud moved from the right side of the sky to the left. As it shifted, it grew darker, creepier, and more intense. People followed and began to amass on the left side at the top of the quarry, a high cliff. Confusion set in, and those closest to the edge fell off. We watched as they tumbled down into the water. Some also fell over the opposite edge. Those in the back of the crowd didn't see what was happening and continued to press forward. Ones who were penned up front began screaming when they realized they were about to be herded off the cliff. Sadly, so many packed onto the rim that the ground started to break away. Then, pandemonium set in as it collapsed, spilling people in every direction.

The chaos snapped some of the people out of the delusion created by the cloud. Finally, they knew it wasn't Jesus but an antichrist. Satan disguised himself with something that appeared to be biblical. He clothed himself in a paradigm that many in the church viewed Jesus and the "end-times" through and deceived them into missing the real Jesus. This pessimistic worldview of eschatology and the goodness of God resulted in many falling away and missing the (fullness of relationship with) real Jesus.

Just when it seemed like all was going dark, a second cloud appeared on the right side of the sky. We could feel power surging from it like a billion electrical currents. It carried a golden hue that sparkled like teardrops on a leaf after a fresh storm. A bright light burst from the center.

I awakened to the knowledge that this was no cloud. Such a disturbance could not have originated from this world. Heaven was emerging before us as the expanse filled the sky.

The prophet began yelling, "Jesus is coming. Jesus is coming!" When the people recognized the authenticity of the prophecy, the cloud moved to the center of the sky, driving out the first cloud and the shadow it had cast over the left side of the quarry.

The center of the expanse was right in front of me now, bringing greater clarity and detail. It was massive and awesome. It seemed to be the very center of the universe and all existence. What I saw was much bigger than the Earth or the sky.

Peering into a greater, all-encompassing realm, the sight before me intensified. The more I was able to take in, the more it expanded. The encounter itself was interacting with my level of absorption. Its appearance was dazzling. It sparkled and shimmered. There were golden tones throughout that seemed to be alive. The outer edge was a darker gold, rich and dense. It looked ancient, and I felt as if it contained the history of the universe. The closer I looked towards the center, the golden hue was much lighter and brighter. There were interworking's of gold and bright white, almost like a luminescent fabric that vibrated in waves of glistening life. The vibrations were heard in eternity past, present, and future—harmonizing all of space and time.

The feeling this cloud gave was seducing. I had to look; I had to experience and behold what was before me. It drew me. I felt "more alive" than at any other time in my life. As my eyes continued toward the center of the cloud, I knew what awaited me. It was a moment of unveiling. In order to look, my heart would be on full display. I didn't feel shame; rather, safety and comfort. I knew that in looking, my heart would be protected. I felt the awesomeness of the moment. There was a fear unlike the feeling produced by the first cloud. This fear was like the feeling on my wedding day, which culminates in the intimacy of oneness. It was blissful and intoxicating. It was the understanding that the destination of my sight was the center of the expanse, Who dwelled there, and the intimate union that gently awaited my gaze.

It was light outside as rays of sunshine replaced the shadows of the former cloud. The sun, in its strength, causes you to squint, even upon emerging from a brightly lit room. As I transferred my gaze from the sky to the center of the cloud, I had the same sensation. Yet, the intensity of the light didn't burn my eyes. Although I had the instinct to shield them, there was no need because the light was accessible to my sight. It invited me to look and see.

The entire array was an instantaneous interaction as my eyes accelerated toward the Source of the light—Jesus Himself, hovering in the middle of the sky, shining like a supernova in the golden expanse. It reminded me of the description of the mobile throne in Ezekiel.

He was so magnificently bright that I struggle to describe it. I had to fight to focus on his form through layers of white light that exuded from His being. To quickly glance upon Him was to see brilliance and whiteness. Gazing upon Him was like focusing on one of those three-dimensional pictures that you must look at intently to see the hidden image. Once you see it, the picture pops out.

An endless countenance surrounded Him. There was more depth, texture, and reality inside of the expanse than on the outside. It was like peering into an eternal door. I gazed into true reality. In Him, I viewed everything—time, space, eternity—all at once.

Decades after this dream, I continue to discover greater depth, details, and insight than ever before. It is as if the dream was a gift that I get to take with me for the rest of my life, and every time I open it, there is something new and exciting never seen before. When I first had the dream, I had no words for the beauty of Jesus in the expanse. Now, when I recount the scene, it's as if I go back into the experience to take a look around at everything that was happening at that moment. To this day, words still fail to describe Jesus or recreate the weight of the impact of seeing Him in such a bright display. I cannot describe His form or His face. I still look intently at Him to find features hidden in His radiance. It's like looking at the sun and trying to describe the surface to you—how the gases move, and solar flares jump here and there, or the collection of colors swirling around. I simply ask Jesus to take you into an encounter as you read this so you, too, can experience the brightness of His countenance, shining in His heavenly place.

As the cloud came to rest at the focal point in the sky, it captured the attention of the entire church. All eyes were on Jesus. Each of us engaged in individual yet united encounters. We had a collective awareness. The time that passed from the appearance of the expanse to its moving to the sky's center was only a few seconds. Everything I have described occurred within those moments. As I stared at the Son, all earthly limitations faded away. I found myself right in front of the King of the Universe.

In the next moment, a stunning flash of light sparked next to me. I watched in amazement as Brandon flew out into the center of the expanse like a rocket blasting off and exploded into a massive fireball. It was like watching a missile-firing into the sun. As he flew, a trail of yellow light, like the tail of a comet, followed him. It looked like a fiery substance engulfed him with a white-hot interior. His destination was Jesus. He flew right into Him. In an instant, Brandon was hovering mid-air, slightly to the right of Jesus, just as moments before, he was sitting slightly to the left of the prophet. What I was watching happen in Heaven was mirroring what was happening on the Earth, forming a circle.

Encountering Jesus transfigured his appearance. His arms sprouted wings and were raised straight out on each side. He was glowing and awesome in appearance. He looked like a heavenly being yet retained his humanity. It was a marriage of natural and supernatural, earthly and divine. There were layers of light encircling him, almost as if he was in a bubble of purity and light. He seemed to carry an environment around him, just as Jesus did when He appeared. Growth and expansion vibrated as he took his place in the sky as a son of God. True sonship is born in the presence of the Son. He looked over the Earth from his newfound heavenly seat with eyes to see as Heaven sees and a heart on fire with love.

All of this happened in a flash. The details were imprinted in my mind like an x-ray while moving rapidly through the events during the dream. I was awestruck by his ascent. It released something within me at the speed of light. No sooner had he flown into the cloud before I felt my spirit begin to detonate. I found my ignition skyward. It was a rush of pure adrenaline. "I knew that I knew" I would make it. The question of flight, gravity and natural law did not even cross my mind, nor did the thought of falling even occur to me. Instead, a storm of belief baptized my being. It was such a state of transcendence that my only viable response was to fly.

I may have had a taste of the array of emotions and faith Peter experienced just as he stepped onto the sea. The moment was irresistible. Peter saw with true sight, knowing it was safer on the water with Jesus than in the boat. Likewise, it was better for me to ride the clouds with Jesus than to sit on the rock face. There was no instruction manual. All I had to navigate was to follow Brandon's ascent. I was compelled to launch. I lit up the mushroom cloud of a nuclear explosion and flew into the expanse, into the realm of heaven, and collided with the Person of Jesus.

It was so quick yet so expansive that the moment of impact was almost beyond articulation. I had an encounter with Jesus in which an explanation of this is beyond my ability to write. Instantly, I exploded into a fireball, just like Brandon. We were floating in the sky, with Heaven and Earth as our dwellings. I was on one side of Jesus, and Brandon was on the other. Again, similar to a few moments before when we were on either side of the prophet—a parallel. The natural scene is who we are in everyday life as part of the Body of Christ, but the supernatural scene is who we really are as part of the Heavenly Family.

The prophet represents the Ministry Gifts given to equip the church for the works of ministry in Ephesians 4:11. He phased into Jesus and back as a representation of the heavenly scene. An apostolic team flowing in fullness will have Jesus as their only agenda. They will recognize and prepare the church for His appearing. "The spirit of prophecy is the testimony of Jesus." Prophecy at this level pierces the heart with the perfection of Jesus. Our response was a genuine Jesus encounter.

Next, my peripheral vision expanded, and I could see all around. I was aware of the enormity and complexity of the situation. We were no longer viewing something "above and beyond" us. Instead, the encounter absorbed us, sucking us into the vacuum of irresistibility. We became characters in the movie. We were no longer viewing Heaven from Earth; we were now viewing Earth from Heaven. "Above and beyond" became the "here and now."

I also had outstretched wings, yet I could still feel my hands. It was like having both together, or one or the other, available as needed. Waves of electricity and fire pulsated throughout my body. It was a cognizance of life unlike anything I have ever known. I knew I was alive before, but now I was alive in the fullness of union with Jesus. This is who I've always been, yet the encounter unlocked the true identity Jesus had stored in my DNA.

My ascent became the catalyst for our two remaining friends to join us in the sky. I watched as they flew into the expanse like surface-to-air missiles. There were four of us now positioned where Heaven meets Earth, hovering to the right and the left of the King of Majesty. It felt like Family. Each of us had a different color flame, representing our unique gifts and how we affect the Earth, both as individuals and as a team. It reminds me of the Voltron cartoon. Separate, they were powerful but united they were unstoppable. As impressive as I felt before, the feeling was even more exhilarating with all four of us. It was like a power surge as their energy increased my own. My mental capacity was unlocked, and I knew all of my thoughts and connected telepathically with their thoughts. Love, honor, and respect for them arose in my heart. I burned with passion for them, and I could feel their love for me. Spirit and truth connected us. Nothing would be impossible for us in this formation.

From our place in the sky, we could see the top of the rock quarry—church. Beyond it was a thick blackness. Out from the dark multitudes were streaming over the edge into the church. As all of us became aware of this, our mission downloaded into our hearts, and without hesitation, we flew out into the darkness, fanning out into different directions.

The further I went into the darkness, the darker it became. Even though it was pitch black, I could still see. There were people below me going through their daily lives. The light of Christ was shining through me. I watched as His light illuminated them and eliminated the darkness. They began moving in the direction of the church. I looked back and saw that the trail of fire following me had lighted up the path. There were now multitudes rushing to freedom.

Even from this distance, I could see Jesus above the sky, enthroned in majesty. Once His light pierced their hearts, they went straight into the rock quarry. Amazingly, everyone seemed to make it. Not one turned back towards the darkness after beholding His light.

A revolution was taking place.

As I looked, I saw flashes of light launching into the sky from the quarry and exploding into fireballs. They were experiencing Jesus just as we had and lighting the way to Jesus and sending as many as they could find into the church to become disciples. The new believers would sit in fellowship next to the prophet until they matured into their destiny. Once they could fly, they were also sent to fulfill the apostolic commission. So, there was a pattern of people coming out of the darkness into the light and encountering Jesus. Next, they flew back out into the night to send even more people into the light. This cycle went on from generation to generation, ever-increasing and ever-expanding.

My last glimpse revealed the spreading of the light and the growth of the church. The areas behind me that were once dark were now light and continued to push back the darkness in front of me. The celestial landscape of heaven and earth revived in the light as kingdom family took their rightful place in the heavenlies.[83]

The dream is a picture of the church doing life with Jesus throughout the ages. It fills and fills until the light has encircled the earth, and darkness has died. So, this dream, too, had a timeless element, but it was a view of heaven and earth beyond the veil. God is mystifying and mesmerizing. He sustains the furthest parts of the universe, the beginning, and end of time, yet one glance from you fills His heart with love, as He loves us right where we are.

---

[83] David Edwards, *The Call for Revivalists* (Atlanta: Revivalism, 2012, 2018), p.49-60.

Activation

1. Ask God to ignite your dream life. Dreams are where God can show us things our minds cannot comprehend. As we explore them, we experience metanoia, empowering us to a new level of faith when we are awake.

2. God longs to unveil (apocalypse) things to us. "For the Lord, God does nothing without revealing his secret to his servants, the prophets (Amos 3:7 ESV)." Pray for Him to reveal the heavenly realm to you. It's key to record our dreams and prophetic experiences. I recommend writing them down in a journal or recording them on audio. We also have a *Prophetic Pictures, Words, and Dreams Journal* available to assist you in your journey.[84]

---

[84] See resource page.

GODSPEED

The past 21 chapters of the "Mystify Series" (ten here and eleven in Mystify) have built upon each other, not as steps, but as layers of glass, through which I hope you will see God in a new way. This approach reveals the pattern through which He has moved in my life and how the Bible reveals the blueprint for experiencing God.

As writers do, a threequel may emerge on the Majesty of God. But no promises just yet as manuscripts of Kingdom Family and Awakening burn within me. Wherever my writing takes me, it will spiral outward from here. I believe these two books mark a transition from my first ten years as an author to the next. Misunderstood, criticized, or praised, I lay at His feet in awe that I had such stories to tell. And even more thankful that I get to share them with you.

I pray you see the biblical library as a cohesive invitation for more. It was written to reveal the story of God. When we apprehend it from the literary, cultural, and historical context of the authors, we find that the story is layered in the supernatural worldview in which they lived. The supernatural was just as real to them as the natural, and they had an unfolding collection of literature, history, and narrative standing as an eternal testament of who God was to them and who He is for us today. He never changes, and His heart is for all of His children to experience Him in all the ways He makes Himself available.

Each of our stories will be unique, grounded in the principles of His word, and a testimony to our generation of the love, kindness, and power of Jesus in us through the Holy Spirit. So may my story inspire yours!

> And the Lord answered me, "Write the vision; make it plain on tablets, so he may run who reads it."
>
> Habakkuk 2:2 ESV

AUTHOR

David Edwards is the Sr. Leader of Awaken Family Church and the Director of School of Revivalists. He lives with Allessia, his bride and ministry partner of over 20 years, and their doggy Rylee in Santa Rosa Beach, FL. He is a graduate of Fire School of Ministry and author of nine books.

Follow the links below for more information about their church, school, and ministry:

- awakenfamilychurch.com

- schoolofrevivalists.com

- facebook.com/davidedwardsofficial

- instagram.com/thedavide

- youtube.com/daefire1

Ministry Invitations

David & Allessia travel and speak at churches and conferences. If you would like to find out more about inviting them to your event (scan qr code).

School of Revivalists is a college of ministry designed to identify, activate, equip, and release the sons and daughters of God to transform all spheres of society. We emphasize the presence of God, biblical excellence, the activation and practice of the spiritual gifts, outreach and evangelism, prophetic development, leadership and communication training, and much more!

We offer a dynamic curriculum that allows students to graduate each year of completion and receive a diploma or degree based on their previous level of study.

Programs

- **Certificate in Transformation Coaching**
- **Diploma in Kingdom Ministry**
- **Associate & Bachelor in Kingdom Theology**
- **Master in Ministry (MMin)**

We also offer kingdom apprenticeships, ordination, advanced ministry training, and more. Learn at your own pace in the SOR Virtual Academy, a monthly membership program. For more info, to apply for one of our programs, or check out our E-Courses, visit schoolofrevivalists.com (scan qr code).

BOOKS

By David & Allessia Edwards

The Call for Revivalists

Activating a Prophetic Lifestyle

Radical Purity

Revivals & Revivalists

Sky Dream

Prophetic Pictures, Words, & Dreams Journal

Mystify Series

Mystify

Mesmerize

Everstill,

Allessia,

You are My Delight!

www.ingramcontent.com/pod-product-compliance
Lightning Source LLC
Chambersburg PA
CBHW060915140726
47996CB00001B/253